Melbourne Circle

WALKING, MEMORY and LOSS

'*Melbourne Circle: Walking, Memory and Loss* is a very special book. Just read it, and then take to the streets and walk with the same spirit of enquiry.'

– Sophie Cunningham, *The Age*

'A beautiful meditation on the streets in which we live, ghosts, love and loss ... While there is sadness in this book, Gadd writes with warmth, humour and a generosity of spirit.'

– Stephen Romei, *The Weekend Australian*

'An endearing book about enduring love and serendipitous discoveries; of remnants of the past pasted onto old buildings, and the way these ghost signs are portals into another time.'

– *The Saturday Paper*

'What a gem this book is! Oddity, wonderment, weirdness, radical attention: these splendid essays reveal a marvellous Melbourne most of us have never encountered before.'

– Gail Jones, author of *Five Bells* and *The Death of Noah Glass*

ALSO BY NICK GADD

Ghostlines
Death of a Typographer

Nick Gadd is the author of the novels *Death of a Typographer* (shortlisted for a Ned Kelly Award in 2020) and *Ghostlines* (winner of a Ned Kelly Award in 2009 and a Victorian Premier's Literary Award for an Unpublished Manuscript in 2007). Nick was the winner of the 2015 Nature Conservancy Australia Nature Writing Prize, and his non-fiction has appeared in *Griffith Review, Meanjin, Kill Your Darlings* and *The Guardian*. His interests include psychogeography, typography and urban wandering. Find more of his work at melbournecircle.net and nickowriter.com.

WALKING,
MEMORY
and LOSS

Nick Gadd

ARCADIA

Published 2020 by Arcadia
the international general books' imprint of
Australian Scholarly Publishing Ltd
7 Lt Lothian St Nth, North Melbourne, Vic 3051
Tel: 03 9329 6963 / Fax: 03 9329 5452
enquiry@scholarly.info / www.scholarly.info

ISBN 978-1-922454-07-2

Cover Art: Jim Pavlidis

For Lynne

CONTENTS

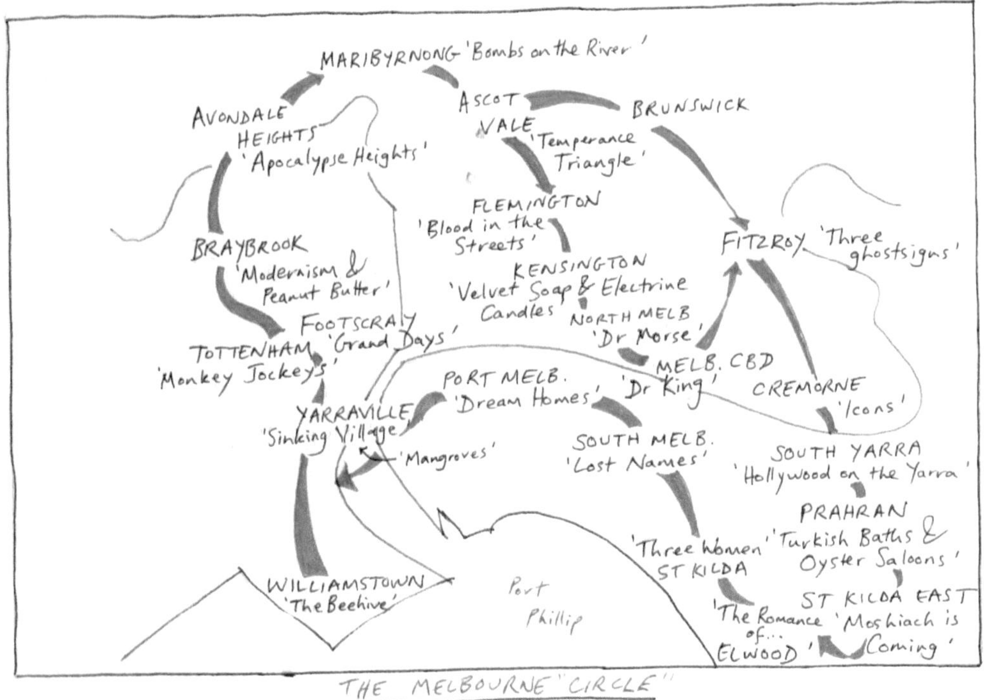

In writing these stories of Melbourne's recent history, I acknowledge that the original and traditional owners of the land on which Melbourne is built are the Boon Wurrung and Woi Wurrung (Wurundjeri) peoples of the Kulin Nation.

A NOTE ABOUT THE MAPS

The maps in this book serve two purposes: to indicate the routes that we followed on our walks; and to suggest points of interest that readers may like to visit for themselves. The maps are personal and incomplete, and intended to provide an impression only of each location.

‘You take delight not in a city’s seven or seventy wonders, but in the answer it gives to a question of yours.’ – Italo Calvino

‘Grief turns out to be a place none of us know until we reach it.’ – Joan Didion

PROLOGUE

PARISH OF CUT PAW PAW, COUNTY OF BOURKE

I came across our certificate of title while I was sorting out the estate after you died. Life ultimately boils down to a matter of a few documents in the eyes of the law: birth certificate, marriage certificate, bank statements, will, death certificate. I hadn't looked at it since 1994, when we bought our first home. It's a pompous document, with the Victorian coat of arms at the top, and the words 'Certificate of Title' printed in a Gothicky font. Underneath, amidst the legal lingo ('an Estate in Fee-simple subject to the Encumbrances noted hereunder') someone from the Titles Office had typed in the following details on a governmental Remington: 'Lot 338 on Plan of Subdivision No. 11691 ... Part of Crown Allotment 6 Portion 6 Section 8 Parish of Cut Paw Paw County of Bourke'. It's dated 'the Eighteenth day of July One thousand nine hundred and fifty-five', and there's a tiny diagram of the property with measurements in feet and inches. Oddly, nowhere does it state our actual address. According to this certificate, we lived in 'Parish of Cut Paw Paw County of Bourke'.

The names puzzle me. I had no idea that Melbourne had 'parishes' let alone 'counties'. And if you'd asked me to name the ones we lived in, I'd have been stumped, despite having resided here for twenty-five years. According to the website of the Living Museum of the West, 'Cut Paw Paw' may be derived from 'Koort Boork Boork' meaning 'clump of she-oaks' in the language of the people of the Kulin nation. The name Cut Paw Paw hearkens back, inaccurately, to the voices of the original owners, and the living trees that once covered their land, before it became 'an Estate in Fee Simple' in the language of the invaders. The other name on this certificate, Bourke, refers to Richard Bourke, the Governor of New South Wales, who proclaimed the town of Melbourne in 1837, and thus got large chunks of it named after himself. You and I, though, never thought of ourselves as living in the 'Parish of Cut Paw Paw County of Bourke'. To us, it was our first home, a little weatherboard place in Yarraville, with a gum tree, a shed, and a Hills Hoist in the backyard. Pretty ordinary, but so is most history.

More names appear, crossed out, on the front page. The first owners, Leo Joseph Scott, Carpenter, and Waveney Isabel Scott, Married Woman, took possession in 'one thousand nine hundred and fifty-five'. They were the first to sleep under this roof and to look out of these windows at the new street as it came into being – a few dozen weatherboard houses, all alike, a primary school, a bowling club. They would still have been here when the West Gate Bridge was built, within sight of the house. After the Scotts came William Williams (Foreman) and Kathleen Williams (Home Duties) in the 1970s; then three members of the Moyle family (Robert and Allen, a Technical Assistant and a Boilermaker; and Mavis June, a Married Woman). After them came the bloke who sold the place to us in 1994. Then our names: Nicholas Gadd, Lynne Carolan. The house already had 40 years of history by the time you and I moved in. Our occupations are not recorded, but if they were, teacher, traveller, reader, feminist, lover, partner would be more appropriate for you than 'Married Woman' – but words like that don't get a guernsey on certificates of title.

For the next 25 years, this was where our stories unfolded. We brought home a couple of tiny babies, sent them to the primary school up the road, and raised two young women. There were long-lived dogs and short-lived goldfish. The gum tree crashed through the roof in the storm of 2002. We knocked down the rickety old shed. (Built by Leo Joseph Scott, carpenter, perhaps? That might have been his tool board, with the ghosts of his saws and hammers painted in silhouette.) We put down pavers where the girls rode their trikes around. We planted a lemon tree and tried to grow tomatoes. I remember the old Greek guy next door, now dead, whose wife was never seen out of doors. He had two hobbies: playing his bouzouki, and reporting violations of parking restrictions. He gave us persimmons from his trees and talked about mythology. On the other side, the black-clad lady who spoke no English spent all day watching the street from her front garden. There were occasional bizarre incidents (that time the fruit bat attacked your mum in the backyard, the very night the girls were watching *Batman*). We celebrated life events: birthdays, festivals, anniversaries, netball finals, end-of-term performances, VCE results. Walked our dogs in the local parks, handed out how-to-vote cards at the primary school on election day, wandered up the road to get a good view of the New Year's Eve fireworks. I remember the laughter and the dancing.

And I remember the stillness that descended on the house when cancer moved in and, exactly seven months later, took you away.

*

Walking together was one of the constants in our relationship. We got together in the 1980s, when I was living in the south of Italy, and our first date involved a long walk around the ruins of Pompeii, a location that's hard to beat for people like us who are interested in uncovering the secrets of the past. You'd always been a traveller, you'd already worked in five different countries, and though I'd not been that adventurous I shared your love of exploring. We became inveterate wanderers through cities like Cairo, Naples, London, Paris, Amsterdam. Much later, after we'd raised our family, the desire to walk took hold again, but now it was our home city that became a subject of fascination. We'd lived in Melbourne twenty-five years, but how well did we know it?

We began taking trains to unfamiliar stations to walk, at random, down laneways, alongside creeks, and behind abandoned factories where taggers and street artists ran riot and hard-eyed men watched us with suspicion. We drifted through drowsy residential suburbs where surreal things manifested at unexpected moments, as if directed by David Lynch. The suburbs are places of layered stories. Most are forgotten, but traces linger for those who want to connect with lost lives. We weren't experts in history, architecture, art, or planning: all we had was our curiosity and our eyes, yours sharper than mine. It turned out that it didn't take a Roman ruin to get us excited: a faded advertising sign or remnants of art deco on a '30s milk bar had the same effect. As Walter Benjamin wrote in *A Berlin Chronicle*: 'To lose oneself in a city – as one loses oneself in a forest – that calls for quite a different schooling. The signboards and street names, passers-by, roofs, kiosks or bars must speak to the wanderer like a crackling twig under his feet.' We were drawn to lost and derelict things: the romantic, neglected, and weird. Sometimes we crossed paths with our younger selves, revisiting places that were part of our own history, remembering our gains and losses. Personal and historical narratives mingled, interwoven with the places themselves. And I began to write about them.

The literature of walking is usually of solitary strollers, mostly male. From Dickens losing himself in nocturnal London, Baudelaire flaneuring around Paris, Kierkegaard roaming Copenhagen, and W.G. Sebald grumping along the paths of East Anglia, to present-day solo-walkers like Robert MacFarlane, the idea is that you do it alone, and have profound thoughts along the way. There have been notable female walkers, like Virginia Woolf, who described her peregrinations in a wonderful essay, 'Street Haunting: a London Adventure'; Rebecca Solnit, who has chronicled her walks around San Francisco and Ireland; and Vivian Gornick in New York. But couples who walk together are rare, at least in books. One example of a joint walking project, although not a particularly encouraging one, is Marina Abramovic and her partner Ulay, who spent three months walking 2000 miles in opposite directions towards each other along the Great Wall of China. On meeting in the middle, they ended their relationship.

Maybe I once thought this would be a solo undertaking, too. But your natural curiosity brought you into the project, and once you get involved in something, you don't let go. I quickly realised that walking with another person is quite different to walking alone, and more satisfying. Choosing the route becomes a joint enterprise, shaped by ongoing negotiation, glances, gestures and words, now one of us taking the lead, now the other. One observes more, and differently, when accompanied by a co-walker. At the end of a day's walk, the things that stuck in your mind were quite different to what had lodged in mine, but it would be strange if that wasn't the case, since everyone's city is different. You might have spotted a curious old bell-pull in a doorway, the fake birds in a cage in a café, traces of deco on a milk bar, the absurd name of a new company on an old factory ('What on earth are Logistical Future Solutions?'), while I'd been tracking Victorian house names and painted soap advertisements. Sometimes we walked quietly, each with our own thoughts, but more often our walking was accompanied by the kind of observations, allusions, in-jokes, teases, references and memories that make up the talk of people who know each other so well they can read each other's mood from a single word or a split second of silence. I wish I could remember more of those conversations, but they are gone now, spent like loose change in the days when we assumed we'd have plenty more. Now I would give anything for a few minutes of the casual chat we tossed to each other like juggling balls.

Being together in a new place creates another memory, forever linking the place and the experience with the other person. So certain cafés, laneways, corners, park benches are irrevocably connected with you. As we went in search of ordinary suburban stories, we were writing our own: the story of two people who found each other, then lost each other, and found each other again. Because we did have some difficult patches. What couple doesn't, over the course of a long relationship? There were times when we drifted apart, a fog descended and we seemed to lose sight of each other. Times when cruel things were said, and stupid mistakes were made. Times when the maps made no sense, and we weren't on the same journey at all. The stress of caring and fixing, and of dealing with other people's sickness and problems sucked the strength out of you until there was nothing left. You said, around 2013, that you had lost your way. I lost mine too, and perhaps that was the only time that either of us imagined a life without the other. But we both knew, deep down, that we were each other's best hope of finding a way out of the fog.

Walking was one of the things that saved us. It helped us find our way back to each other – not to break up, Abramovic-style, but to cling onto each other again, as if for the first time.

*

Gradually, an idea took hold: to circumnavigate the whole city in a rough circle, passing through as many suburbs as possible in a series of connected walks. The inspiration came from the English writer, Robert MacFarlane:

> Psychogeography: a beginner's guide. Unfold a street map ... place a glass, rim down, anywhere on the map, and draw around its edge. Pick up the map, go out into the city, and walk the circle ...

Another model was Iain Sinclair's *London Orbital* which describes a walk along the course of the M25, the motorway that encircles London. The concept was easy to grasp, but harder to achieve. What we ended up with was a circle of sorts, far from perfect: more an erratic wiggly line, with many loops and whorls and doublings-back. Most weekends, on a Saturday or Sunday, you'd say:

– *Let's go psychojogging.*

We started each walk at the point where the previous one had finished, armed with a rough idea of where we wanted to go, but ready to follow our instincts and hunches, to duck down unforeseen alleys and into obscure arcades. Often we'd pass no one else, but when we did encounter others, you had a knack for getting into conversation. I remember that rough-looking bloke, outside a weird little plot of land where old carnival rides were stored, who asked suspiciously what we were up to, and replied to your answer with: 'History? What fuckin' history? People getting murdered, people getting stabbed? That's the only history around here.' But after a few minutes, he softened enough to tell you his own, more peaceful memories. There were others, less abrasive, whom we encountered in the streets, or who came out of their houses to talk to us. After a few months I began a blog about our walks, called *Melbourne Circle*, which attracted a modest readership and comments from people who wanted to share their own stories.

The entire journey took us two years as we wound through

some fifty suburbs – and in each one, we encountered layers of time and the traces of past lives. As we walked, we talked about our own history, the places we'd been and things we'd done, and how our own lives were forever intertwined with these suburbs. Later, when we took our last few walks along Williamstown foreshore, pretending there was still a future although we knew there wouldn't be, you said how much you'd loved those walks, how much we'd learned about the places and ourselves. It was you, of course, who showed me what it was we'd really been doing and what it meant. I've tried to capture some of that in this book.

WILLIAMSTOWN: THE CIRCLE BEGINS

The walk begins here: Nelson Place, Williamstown, July 2014. A cold afternoon, the wind tangy with salt, the sky an icy blue with feathery clouds. Hundreds of yachts are bobbing on the water, their masts a forest of toothpicks. We stand watching as a vessel glides slowly towards the docks, loaded with its Lego-like containers. Berthed at Gem Pier is the HMAS *Castlemaine*, the Royal Australian Navy vessel that is now a museum, and close by is the Greenpeace ship, *Sea Shepherd*, which departs from here to pursue whalers in the Southern Ocean: it's dinged on the hull where the whalers have rammed it. There are pleasure cruisers, power boats, a police launch, and a ferry waiting to take people up the river to Scienceworks, or further on to Southbank and the casino. It doesn't seem likely that high rollers arrive by ferry, but who knows?

Here on shore, it's not very busy. A few kids are swinging from monkey bars on the playground, like our two daughters did fifteen years ago, but there's no one hitting tennis balls on the courts where we used to play. In the park by the pier, we notice rugged-up strollers in puffer coats and beanies, joggers in active wear, and a little dog in a Burberry jacket. A few hardy souls sip cappuccinos from cardboard cups, and an English couple want their photo taken. Others are here for gelato, fish and chips or tandoori chicken; perhaps to get their nails done at one of many nail salons, or a tarot reading at the New Age shop where pashminas flutter in the breeze like pennants. This was once a bustling port: maybe whaling ships departed a hundred years ago from the very same spot that *Sea Shepherd* does today, when the streets were ariot with sailors drinking and brawling at dozens of pubs. In his memoir *The Watcher on the Cast-Iron Balcony*, Hal Porter remembered Nelson Place as full of 'empty taverns and coffee palaces, tumble-down ship-chandlers and providores, deserted brothels, lanes and courts crowded with fennel bushes as high as sailors.' There are still a few boat builders here, but it's mostly gelato, spirituality and nails.

When we look carefully, though, there are in fact traces of that past around us. We spot a faded sign reading 'chandler', and another for a long-gone hardware store. The Gothic signage of the old newspaper, *The Advertiser*, stands out clearly, although the newspaper office has morphed into a bar and grill. On the corner of Ann Street, the Oriental Hotel, built in 1854, is scheduled for demolition. It's festooned with protest signs reading 'Save historic hotel!' and 'Bollocks!', but according to the tribunal that decides these things the hotel is too derelict to be restored, so the protest looks doomed. Along with the vacant land alongside – once occupied by a woollen mill – it's going to be turned into a fancy new development, and there are already promotional signboards proclaiming the amenities of 'Waterline Place'. It's not the only redevelopment: half of the old Bristol Hotel at the top of Ferguson Street is already torn down. Around Williamstown, other old signs here and there hint at its history: Penfolds Sherry, Olympic Cycle Tyres, Licensed Victuallers (who provided food and drink for ships), along with slogans such as 'Greys is Great!' advertising a defunct brand of cigarettes. Other survivors of the lost past include pubs, houses, schools and churches built in the nineteenth century from local bluestone.

Nelson Place leads to the Point Gellibrand lookout, passing en route between Seaworks Maritime Museum on one side and on the other, the Titanic – a theatre restaurant that has inexplicably survived, year after year, longer than the ship it is named after. Soon we reach the Timeball Tower, a small bluestone edifice dating from the 1850s. Every day, the ball at the top of the tower used to be dropped at exactly 1.00 pm, enabling ships in the bay to set their chronometers accurately. We wander around the tower for a while, but this walk isn't about official landmarks, so we move on and stand at the lookout, staring out to sea. From here, we have a view of the city with its rapidly sprouting apartment towers, and across the bay to St Kilda. On the horizon, container vessels are slumbering, in no need of any help from the Timeball Tower. Gulls scrap for chips at our feet while other seabirds skim the green ocean and the occasional pelican drifts overhead.

We turn and make our way back through quiet residential streets. Williamstown's wild days are behind it and the streets have a sleepy genteel air. Men with leaf blowers vainly battle for control over nature. Street-facing walls display little blue plaques that denote places of historical interest. Yes, there are museums to visit, botanical gardens we could stroll through, and perhaps we might step on board the HMAS *Castlemaine*, but what we are seeking is more elusive, humbler ... the kind of history that's unofficial.

In the Williamstown Museum, run by volunteers, there's a heterogeneous collection, like the contents of someone's attic: wind-up gramophones, croquet mallets, footy photos and trophies, formal photos of the Williamstown Centenary Ball 1934, sewing machines, a butter churner, a carved emu egg. You are drawn to a painting of a young woman, a self-portrait, with a biographical note.

> *– Look – she won a travelling scholarship, but her father wouldn't let her go.*

Your face is set in that expression I have come to know very well, and I conclude you are thinking of fathers who try to control their daughters' lives, and of young women who break free and roam the world.

– I want our girls to go everywhere.

We leave the museum and a few minutes later we are heading north along Melbourne Road. At the corner of Russell Place there's a two-storey Victorian building, probably once a shop, now a private residence. In one of the windows there's an installation, not unlike the museum's, made up of random pictures, pennants, books and clutter. But what intrigues us are the copious traces of painted names on the walls. As we're trying to decipher them, a middle-aged, long-haired guy emerges from the front door and tells us that the place has been a hangout for artists and rock'n'roll types since the 1970s. There are funky wooden sculptures in the back yard. But he's heard that, years ago, it was a butcher's shop.

We squint together at the traces of faded paint, which give the place a romantic flavour. The blue is as pale as the sky, the white as wispy as clouds. Gradually, words come into focus: Robur, McAlpin's, Berger master, Kem-tone. I swear I can see 'Empire' on the lower half of the wall. There are more words running along the top, almost too faded to read. On stepping back to get a better view of the signage high on the Russell Place wall, we make out the name 'A. Vowles'. When we cross Melbourne Road to look at the front of the building, we detect the words 'Cheap Cash Grocer' and the name of the building, which can be read on the little curved pediment at the top: 'The Beehive, 1889'. It's like filling out a crossword puzzle. And the answer to one across, running around the entire top of the building, barely discernible, is the phrase 'The Williamstown and Newport Underclothing Depot A. Vowles'.

Years ago, this building would have been a prominent landmark, strategically placed on the main road between Melbourne and Williamstown. Mr Vowles's name would have been visible from far away. Hal Porter must have passed many times – perhaps he even got his undies here. Who, we wondered, was this purveyor of underclothing?

A helpful member of the local history society, back at the museum, gave us some answers. He produced a much-thumbed folder of photocopied pages from street directories, which revealed the names of the owners of the building. Later, we entered their names into Trove, the database of the National Library of Australia, and pieced together more of the story from archived newspapers online.

'The Beehive' (a name suggestive of industry, if not of underwear) was opened in 1889, by Albert Vowles, whose name is still visible at the top of the shop more than a century later. Vowles's previous premises, in Ferguson Street, had burned down in 1888, but he soon bounced back. A local paper, *The Chronicle,* reported on

28 September 1889: 'Mr A Vowles notifies that he will reopen next week the underclothing depot at The Beehive, Melbourne Road.' It must have seemed like a propitious time for a new business. The 1880s were a decade of economic boom – vast amounts of building and expansion were underway, fuelled by speculative investment. However, as tends to happen in Melbourne, it was rapidly followed by a bust, and the 1890s were marked by bankruptcies, bank failures, and unemployment. As it turned out, it wasn't such a great time to be expanding. But the Underclothing Depot was still going in 1900, so Vowles must have survived the economic crisis – I guess he was providing what we would now call an essential service. Pragmatically, he diversified: by 1910, The Beehive was also a grocer's shop, still under the ownership of Vowles. But by 1921 the shop had changed hands and was owned by 'Burgess, grocer and dairy produce.' Sadly, the Williamstown and Newport Underclothing Depot was no more.

Over subsequent decades, the premises became two shops, numbered 164 and 166. One alternated between a grocer's and boot repairer's, while from the late 1920s to the mid-60s, the other was a butcher's. Some time after the 1960s, the artists and musicians moved in and the place took on another new identity, but never lost its external signage. Gradually, the paint has weathered and although some of the names have faded almost to nothing, they still linger, whispering the building's history to those who are willing to listen: Robur tea, McAlpin's flour, Kem-tone paint ...

The AIF Index website, which lists Australians killed in the First World War, gives 164 Melbourne Road as the address of a Charles Brook Burgess, presumably a relative (the son?) of Burgess who ran the grocer's shop, and his peacetime occupation as 'signwriter'. In April 1918, Charles Burgess was killed in action in France, where he was buried. Did he, we wonder, paint some of the older signs on the building – 'cheap cash grocer', 'Robur tea'? Are they a memorial to a young man killed half a world away? There is no way of knowing, but we'd like to think that some of Burgess's work survived.

This is the kind of story we are looking for: small, local, and hiding in plain sight. There is no blue plaque on the wall of Mr Vowles's shop. Instead, he is commemorated by the work of a signwriter, or several, whose careful work adorned his walls more than one hundred years ago. And while thousands of people drive past the building every day, we feel strangely proud and thrilled to know these little snippets of history, as if we are in possession of a secret.

We walk onwards, north towards Newport, the West Gate Bridge looming ahead of us.

MANGROVES

Every time we step outside the front door of our house and look south-east, we can hear the whoosh of traffic from the freeway carrying traffic between Melbourne and Geelong. If we walk a little further up the street, we can see the West Gate Bridge, which connects (and in another way divides) the western and eastern sides of the city. I'm a fan of bridges and I love the lines of this one as it curls across the Yarra, a skipping rope twirled by two kids on opposite banks. But to look at the bridge is to remember its darker story. On a completely ordinary day in October 1970, people in Yarraville, Spotswood and Newport looked up at the crash that reverberated when a span collapsed during the bridge's construction, sending 2000 tons of metal and concrete plummeting into the mud and the river. Among the 35 dead were riggers, ironworkers, and engineers. And boilermakers, like the guy who owned our house. Some of the men were working on the bridge when it fell away beneath them. Life can do that to you sometimes.

Not far from the bridge and right next to the river is the Newport Athletics track, where we used to come every Saturday morning for eight or nine summers while our girls did Little Aths. On the dreaded 'set up mornings', we'd be down there at 7.15 erecting sunshades, hauling equipment trolleys, connecting loudspeakers, and heaving mats into position. The rest of the time we'd be in the long jump pit until midday, raking and measuring, yelling out names to the kids in line ('Aidan! Hayden! Jayden B! *No, not Jayden C!*') while huge brick-shaped vessels made their way to and from the docks, and the runners flew around the track, straining every sinew, and alternating between grimaces and smiles. They could be long, those mornings, especially when rainstorms or heatwaves made them almost unbearable, or windstorms picked up the sunshades and blew them away; but when our girls outgrew Little Aths, and we had our mornings to ourselves again, we missed them. Whenever I pass the track I think of those days, and glance involuntarily towards the long jump pit.

If we go down to the western side of the bridge early in the morning, it's a good place to watch the sun rise behind the city. One morning, you and I were doing just that when a bloke in fluoros with a stubby of beer wandered past. You started chatting to him and he told us he'd worked in construction all over Australia, but whenever he was in Melbourne he came to the bridge to drink to the men who lost their lives. Their names are recorded on a plaque on the base of one of the supports, where the bridge crosses Douglas Parade. There are thirty-five sculpted blocks in a row, each commemorating one of the dead. But the informal gesture of this stranger – too young to have been born in 1970 – struck us as equally moving.

> – *He didn't even know them, but he comes here to remember them.*

Under the West Gate Bridge, there's a forest of mangroves (*avicennia marinara*), which can grow in salty coastal water. We walk down and stand among them, our boots squelching in the ooze, and touch the tough green leaves, while marvelling at the breathing roots that stick up like snorkels. I associate mangroves with the tropics, but apparently it's not that rare to find them this far south. What *is* rare is to find them in a place so industrial, under a freeway, at the mouth of a creek that regularly has toxic crap dumped into it. But they didn't just spring up here naturally. The original mangroves were planted in the 1980s by a local conservationist, and today there's an extensive forest across the backwash, where the river flows into Port Phillip Bay. It took persistence and determination, by the mangroves and the people who planted them, as many plants died in 'pollution events' before the forest really established itself. If there can be a revival of nature in a place like this, if life can bloody-mindedly renew itself in such unpromising circumstances, then it can happen anywhere.

You don't talk a lot about your childhood, but I know that it was tough. I know your dad was an angry man whose hail-fellow-well-met persona was a public front. I know your family life was punctuated by explosions of madness and rage. I know that, in the absence of real parenting, you took on that role for your younger siblings. I didn't hear about this for years though. When I first met you, what drew me to you was your optimism – that was what I fell in love with. How did your eagerness to see and do and live and love grow from such a beginning? Like a mangrove, you evolved to thrive in difficult surroundings. You found a way to get oxygen out of the swamp, you dealt with the salt and the toxic crap, you grew tough leaves and breathing roots, and in the end you flourished.

Throughout our walks, this is a quality we see again and again: alongside the loss and devastation, there is evidence of survival and renewal. From a distance of five years, it is to these signs of hope I most often return.

THE SINKING VILLAGE

And so we reach our own suburb, Yarraville, Parish of Cut Paw Paw, County of Bourke. In 1994, when we moved in, it was already trendifying, a process that intensified over the succeeding years. In those days there were lots of Greek cake shops, a busy Orthodox church, and mysterious little shop fronts where old men played cards sitting at tables. Bradmill, the big clothing factory not far from our house, was still in business and employing some of our neighbours. The Sun Theatre, having closed in the 1980s, was boarded up and near derelict. Most of the local pubs dished up meat and two veg, and beer served by topless barmaids, but some had begun to provide a more diverse range of food options and even *a cappella* nights. Though only ten minutes' drive from the city, Yarraville had the feel of a small town, along with a club for trugo, the local game invented in the 1930s by railway workers in Newport. We went along to an open day once, when our kids were little: you laughed as you whacked a rubber ring with a mallet backwards between your legs at a distant target (women were supposed to use the more ladylike 'sideswipe' technique, but you disdained that option). There was also the Mouth Organ Band, created during the Depression as a low-cost hobby for young people to give them something to do; Rita's legendary deli (whose owner claimed to be related to Mother Teresa); and the servo where you took our car for years, despite its ominous sign reading 'Mechanic on Duty. Drinks, Smokes, 24 hours.'

During the next twenty years, two phenomena unfolded in parallel: the decline of manufacturing, as successive governments stripped away tariffs and jobs were sent offshore; and rapid gentrification, with a consequent increase in property prices. We watched as factories became apartments, wool stores and mills became art spaces, and most of the cake shops and old men's clubs became hip cafés and restaurants. (The old men took to roaming the streets, or sitting in solemn rows on benches, passing senatorial judgement on issues of the day.) The Sun Theatre was renovated and reopened, along with the Sun bookshop. Bradmill closed, causing the loss of hundreds of jobs.

But some things remained the same. At Easter, we watched the Greek community parade through the streets, a priest at the front, the faithful carrying a cross and a bier covered with flowers, choristers chanting '*kyrie eleison*', and hundreds of followers with lighted candles, ranging from old ladies in wheelchairs to tiny kids. Smaller community groups have survived too. Always seemingly on the verge of closure, the trugo club struggles on, year after year, and the Mouth Organ Band continues to play, its waistcoated members appearing at community festivals to perform jaunty versions of *If You Knew Susie*. The oval is busy all year round with footy and cricket. Over the years, we have come to love the traditions of the place, its sense of community and its dash of eccentricity.

Trendy it may have become, but Yarraville never used to be fashionable. This side of the river was where, for generations, stuff was dug up, boiled down, or manufactured: bluestone, meat, hides, sugar, glass, fertiliser, clothes, bombs. These industries, which the whole city depended on, provided the inner western suburbs with its proudly working-class identity during the nineteenth and twentieth centuries. In the early 1990s, when we moved here, I was studying education at Melbourne Uni, and one of my classmates said, 'Yarraville? Where's that? I've never heard of it! It must be a new suburb.' About 150 years old, actually ... but new to her, whose blood was pure eastern suburbs. But even then, Yarraville had begun to be mentioned in property supplements. It was happening in cities across the western world, including Melbourne, as suburbs that formerly belonged to the industrial working class succumbed to gentrification.

And when we moved in, although those old industries were largely in decline or gone, their history was everywhere. It was in the signage that lingered for Patternmakers and Engineers and Chemicals. It was on the walls of the pharmacy, where multiple faded names were visible on top of each other, weathered by the years. It was in the bluestone cobbles of the station car park, formerly a goods yard. It was everywhere we looked.

Just down the road from our house is the still vacant Bradmill factory. After the factory closed, the building was sold to a property developer. He had the land rezoned for residential use, but then did nothing with it, awaiting a suitably huge financial offer: years later, it's still vacant, apart from mysterious characters who occasionally light fires within. We ventured in there once – it wasn't hard, the fence gaped in a dozen places. Inside the cavernous space, our feet crunched on shards of glass, while a million pigeons flapped around in indignation. Painted arrows pointed the way to The Chemical Store and The Proofing Plant. Nature was quietly reclaiming the site: weeds clumped around doorways and sidled up staircases, and rabbits skipped around the vacant land. We came across a burnt-out car full of ash. Unknown artists had painted the walls with crude totemic figures: a naked woman with antlers, a knight brandishing a decapitated head. After the mill closed, there were persistent stories about imminent development, so we expected bulldozers, graders, builders. But nothing much happened. Instead the site waits, poised between its industrial past and its post-industrial future, neither one thing nor the other ... just vague terrain.

Other changes were less obvious, and did not always involve unwanted loss. For example, our local park – Cruickshank Park – was created by a determined community group in the 1970s on the site of a disused quarry, and is now a tranquil place where Stony

Creek flows lined by gums and willows. Along the wharves and beside the river, buildings once housing chemical and fertiliser plants have been demolished but left an indelible mark, as the land stands vacant. It seems many secrets are buried in the earth, and rarely spoken of.

Some secrets lie even closer to home. Before we put down the deposit on our place, you asked one of the building guys at the TAFE where you worked to come and check it out for us. 'Yarraville?' he said. 'Not near the Sinking Village, is it?' It was the first we'd heard of what we discovered is a cautionary tale in construction departments.

Here's the short version. Two decades before we bought our little bit of Yarraville, another bunch of home buyers, most of them of pension age, had the same ambition. In 1973, a number of 'luxurious modern villas' were sold on a block of land at the corner of High Street and Williamstown Road. The units were brand new, brick, had all the mod-cons, and were within walking distance of the shops. The residents moved in, anticipating a pleasant retirement. Within a few weeks, cracks appeared in the units – not the small 'settling down cracks' as the real estate agent reassuringly put it, but gaping chasms through which slices of sky could be seen. Then came the Biblical rains of February 1973 that turned Melbourne's Elizabeth Street into a river: a torrential downpour, yes, but you would expect a new house to cope. Instead, the units crumbled.

The media soon picked up the story. 'I was lying in bed about 5 o'clock one morning when there was this terrible crash,' Mrs Vera Minter, 76, told *The Age*. 'Half the back of the house fell down, there were bricks everywhere.' It happened across the whole estate. The underground plumbing sank, ripping out water and sewerage connections. Windows shattered, driveways split. Residents took to wearing safety helmets so that if walls collapsed, they wouldn't be brained by flying bricks. The site 'looked like a scene from the London blitz', according to Ben Hills, an investigative reporter. The residents had not been told that their dream homes were on top of an abandoned quarry filled with toxic sludge.

So, twenty years after moving into our home, we walk a few hundred metres up the road to check out the Sinking Village.

*

Trucks whomp past us on Francis Street and Williamstown Road as we walk to the site of the Sinking Village: this is still an industrial part of town, although there are curfews on heavy vehicles at night. We're in our usual psychojogging gear: comfortable rather than stylish. You favour jeans and runners, a jacket in your favourite blue-green colour, and you are toting that small backpack that has accompanied you all over the world. It has been with you down the Champs Elysees and around the Pyramids, but now it's passing a sad little establishment with signs reading GIFTS FLOWER and GIFTS SHOP and a symbolic display of withering chrysanthemums, opposite the Quick N Clean Car & Dog Wash which (in contrast) seems to be doing good business. We walk past the supermarket, with its oddly elevated car park that requires a ramp to enter, to the little park with a few scrubby trees, a bench that no one sits on and a playground where no one plays. A row of apartments clings to the park's western edge, and on the southern side are two churches, one for Baptists and one for Mormons, outside which earnest young men in suits can be seen conferring. The park is almost opposite the Yarraville Oval, which formerly used this patch of ground for overflow parking on match days. There are a couple of tennis courts, and a skate park, and the Yarraville Mouth Organ Band is close by, its troupe of elderly blowers still keeping the music alive. We stand in the middle of the park, look at each other and shrug. There is no physical reminder of the Sinking Village, though it is hardly the sort of event local councils are likely to celebrate with a plaque.

– How on earth did it happen? Did everyone just ... forget?

Everything starts with the land. The western suburbs are built on a plain of basalt. When you step onto a park or reserve or the banks of a creek, you feel lumps of it beneath your feet, which explains why quarrying was the area's first industry. An 1860 map of Yarraville includes the promotional copy: 'There is a never failing Creek of Fresh Water at the southern boundary of the township, and the finest building Stone is available within a mile.' Maybe that's how Stony Creek, which flows through Yarraville, got its name. Over the next few decades, many tons of bluestone were dug and dynamited out of local quarries for public buildings and houses across the city. When the quarrying industry declined, the sites were abandoned and subsequently used for waste disposal. In 1900, a local councillor complained, 'Since the plague scare commenced people were sending all manner of rubbish to the tip, which was in a disgraceful condition.' (The *plague*? In *Yarraville*!?) But nothing was done about it. Photographs from the aerial survey of 1945 show quarries pockmarking the western suburbs. Two of them are plainly visible on Williamstown Road, facing each other like lungs: one black, one white.

The old quarries hung around for years, filling up with water and rubbish: older residents still remember people drowning in them. Some were landfilled in the 1970s, and turned into civic amenities. The parks where we walk our dogs, and where people run around playing footy and cricket and hockey, were created on top of abandoned quarries.

But that's not what happened to the site of the quarry on Williamstown Road. When it was no longer economically viable, it was abandoned like the others, until someone decided it would be a great place to dump tons of sludge from the sugar factory. After being 'filled and levelled off' in 1959, the site was used as a transport depot, and also the spot where a travelling circus used to pitch its tents. Then it passed into the hands of a developer who somehow got permission to build a bunch of apartments there. Thus, the stage was set for the sinking village fiasco. The suburb that had produced fine bluestone for splendid public buildings became notorious for units that collapsed within weeks of being completed.

Who was responsible for the disaster? The council blamed the developer, who claimed he had followed regulations; the council said it had surveyed the site and found nothing wrong; the surveyor admitted he was 'not very well up in geology'; the insurance company stated that the residents were not covered for this kind of event; the state government said it was a matter for the local council. The residents had nowhere to go and no way to save their homes.

Like a monument to ignorance, the 'sinking village' stood for several years – pending legal action – before finally being demolished. The land has been devoid of buildings ever since, apart from a little row of apartments that has somehow sprouted on its eastern edge. It took several years, but the residents eventually won some compensation, barely adequate given the trauma they'd been through. But the story still boggles the mind. How was it that in a matter of a few decades, such a crucial piece of knowledge – there's a big hole there, full of sludge – was simply forgotten? To that, I have no answer.

It's not the only place around here with subterranean secrets. Just next door to the park is the Yarraville Plaza. Despite the pretentious name, it's one of those boring retail spaces: a car park flanked on two sides by a chicken shop, a deli, a video shop (closed), a bottle shop, a pharmacy, and a supermarket. There is something odd about it, though. Why this elevation, when the land around is so flat? And why are the (few) trees all in boxes, rather than in the ground?

From the 1920s to the 50s, this site was occupied by Leggo's, a manufacturer of herbicides and pesticides that proudly spruiked itself as 'the largest producer of arsenic in the Southern hemisphere'. After Leggo's closed, the site stood empty until a developer applied for permission to build a supermarket there in the 1990s. The Environment Protection Authority conducted an audit, revealing that it was heavily polluted with pesticide waste, especially arsenic. The solution – or 'remediation' as the EPA calls it – was to cap the site with compacted clay. The groundwater was also found to be contaminated, but the auditor concluded that it was 'unlikely' to reach the nearby creek for fifty years. I don't know whether this was an accurate scientific estimate or a wild guess, but it sounds both comfortingly remote and a suspiciously round number.

These days, thousands of people come and go from the supermarket with little idea that they are buying their cornflakes on top of an arsenic site. But humans tend not to notice anything below ground level. As the English nature writer Helen Macdonald wrote in *H is for Hawk*:

> We are very bad at scale. The things that live in the soil are too small to care about; climate change too large to imagine. We are bad at time, too. We cannot remember what lived here before we did; we cannot love what is not. Nor can we imagine what will be different when we are dead.

We continue along the street beside the arsenic site in a more subdued frame of mind. Sometimes Australian history seems to depend on the collective belief that everything will be fine if we cover it up and forget about it. It seems like a metaphor for so much.

THE OTHER RIVER

Most of Yarraville isn't really on the Yarra. Its eastern boundary borders Melbourne's 'other' river, the Maribyrnong, just before it meets the Yarra, and together they enter Port Phillip Bay. The watercourse that actually flows through Yarraville is Stony Creek, little more than a concrete storm drain for much of its way, which wiggles through the western suburbs before ending up at the backwash among the mangroves. But Stonyville wouldn't have sounded quite so inviting to homebuyers. Perhaps that's what inspired someone – an inventive real estate agent anticipating land sales? – to come up with 'Yarraville'.

Like Cut Paw Paw, 'Maribyrnong' is based on Aboriginal words, meaning 'I can hear a ringtail possum'. But white settlers called the river 'Saltwater' because the tides salt it all the way up to Brimbank. This made it less attractive from the start. If you're establishing yourself in a new place, you want to be near fresh water (i.e. the Yarra). So, from the founding of Melbourne until today, the Maribyrnong (as it became in the early twentieth century in another piece of strategic rebranding) has been 'the Other River'.

It has its uses, though. At the confluence of the two rivers, the deep water was ideal for berthing and loading ships. Wharves were built on the banks of the Saltwater, alongside what is now Whitehall Street, and around them sprang up foundries, smelters, a glue factory, a sugar refinery, an acid works, tanneries and slaughterhouses, and petrochemical and fertiliser plants. The river was used as a drain: industries discharged their effluent into the river and air with impunity (and sometimes still do, in what is politely referred to these days as a 'pollution event'). In 2005, *The Age* reported that the Port of Melbourne, which had bought the site formerly owned by fertiliser company Pivot, had allowed massive quantities of toxic materials to leach into the river. The site had been used to produce chemicals, acid and fertiliser since the 1840s, and tests in the mid-2000s showed that the ground water contained arsenic up to 20,000 times the safe level. According to the terms of the purchase, when the Port bought the site in 2003, Pivot was released from any legal or financial liability to clean it up.

By the early 21st century, when we walk along Whitehall Street, looking across the water towards the petrochemical complex of Coode Island, there have been some changes. Today the acid works stands derelict, though not knocked down. It lingers like the embarrassing drunk at the party that no one wants to talk to, but no one has the guts to throw out. Other premises have been demolished and blocks of land await the next development. Pivot is long gone, but Sugar Australia is still here, and the air is heavy with a strong, treacly odour. Gyprock remains, along with a Mobil refinery and haulage companies. But we can't get too close to the wharves. Before we reach them, we are firmly halted by a wire fence and signs forbidding entry, and soon a Customs and Border Patrol vehicle appears to find out what we are up to. But no such restriction keeps out the rabbits, birds and weeds, which are reclaiming their territory in vacant lots and abandoned factories. Yellow flowering plants burst through wire fences, gutters bow and break under the weight of wild grasses, birds swoop through broken windows to nest in the loading bay, rabbits colonise the workshops. We imagine this place in a thousand years' time, buried by forest, the fences long rusted away ... only a few bricks surviving, and whatever chemical traces lurk in the earth.

You can never step into the same river twice, said the Greek philosopher Heraclitus, because it's not the same river and you're not the same person. In Melbourne, with its history of booms, busts, rushes, bubbles, depressions, and recessions, you never walk down the same street twice. Times of frantic activity are followed by melancholy longueurs when businesses crash, entrepreneurs head for the hills or jail, shops are boarded up, homes repossessed, and the cranes and drills fall silent. Even in normal times, everything changes one way or another. On Moreland Street, close to the river, the Thomas Chemicals building has been converted to apartments, though vestiges of old signage remain, while the Docklands Cotton Mills are occupied by art studios and creatives, and what was once Henderson's piggery is now the Footscray Community Arts Centre.

So here we stand on the western side of the Other River. And if the Maribyrnong is the Other River, everything to the west of it is the Other Side – its industries other, its people other. It's a natural home, then, for many generations of migrants who came to Melbourne over the past half century and more, who have been so relentlessly 'othered' by the media and some politicians. For decades, you taught classes of people from the world's trouble spots, including Vietnam and South America and former Yugoslavia and the Middle East, and most recently the South Sudanese community. They found a home here, and so did we.

What is our connection with the river? We never swim in it or fish in it. Few people do, although the water is cleaner than it used to be. Nor do we sail or row. We go down to its banks sometimes to watch the sun rise behind the city, dazzling shards of light illuminating the stacks of Lego-block containers. We watch massive ships glide like icebergs in and out of the port while we're marshalling kids at the Newport Little Aths track. Sometimes I eat my lunch beside it on warm workdays. And we drive over it a million times on our way into the city or to visit the east. But really, the river is more an idea to us than a body of water. It represents the idea of 'west'. Driving back across the West Gate Bridge – over that body of water, above the mangroves and refineries and container ships, with the level plains of the western suburbs rolling out before us – always feels like coming home.

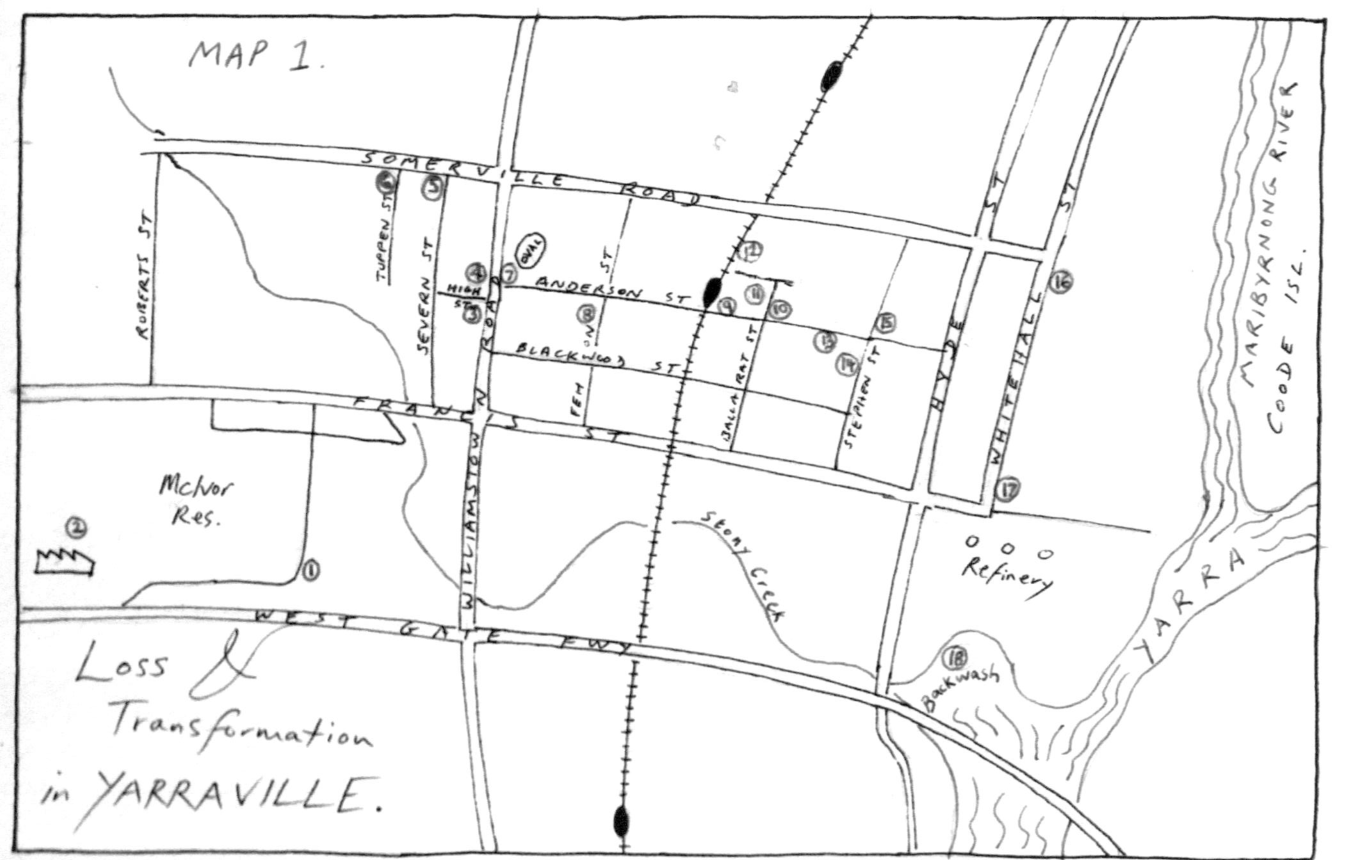
MAP 1.
Loss & Transformation in YARRAVILLE.
SOMERVILLE ROAD
FRANCIS ST
WILLIAMSTOWN ROAD
WEST GATE FWY
ROBERTS ST
TUPPEN ST
SEVERN ST
HIGH ST
ANDERSON ST
BLACKWOOD ST
FEHON ST
BALLARAT ST
STEPHEN ST
HYDE ST
WHITEHALL ST
OVAL
McIvor Res.
Stony Creek
Refinery
Backwash
YARRA
MARIBYRNONG RIVER
COODE ISL.
1
2
3
4
5
6
7
8
9
10
11
12
13
14
15
16
17
18

MAP 1.
LOSS AND TRANSFORMATION IN YARRAVILLE

(1) *The Sun* still rises in the shape of a ghost sign tucked away on a former milk bar. It was Melbourne's morning newspaper until 1990.

(2) The shell of the former Bradmill factory.

(3) The supermarket built on the arsenic site.

(4) The small park that was once the 'Sinking Village' built on an old quarry.

(5) The lost 'Ecks lemonade' ghost sign, now painted over.

(6) An old 'Cash (Grocer?) ...' sign still survives.

(7) Home of the Yarraville Mouth Organ Band, a survivor since the 1930s.

(8) Another survivor, the trugo club behind the Senior Citizens Centre.

(9) Ghost signs for McNish's pharmacy and Bata shoes (along with a cute painted foot).

(10) Pharmacy with layers of ghost signs on its walls.

(11) The restored art deco Sun Theatre.

(12) Once bluestone rail yards, now a car park.

(13) The former Hardies Rubber factory, now apartments, with ghost signs visible. A plumber was based at no. 21.

(14) The former Yarraville Hall, later the Lyric Theatre, now houses a vet and apartments.

(15) The old coffee palace has well-preserved ghost signs on its northern wall.

(16) On Whitehall Street, two contaminated sites include Pivot ...

(17) ... and the acid works.

(18) The backwash, with its forest of mangroves now thriving under the bridge.

GRAND DAYS

In Paisley Street, Footscray, we have often passed a big building with a row of cheap fashion outlets at ground level, and a huge sign above them on the first storey, running the whole length of the building, reading 'Fiesta BINGO'. That's what it used to say, anyway: over the years the sign has gradually fallen apart and now it says something like 'F est BIN O'. It's pretty clear that no one has played bingo there for ages, and the shops aren't thriving either. But behind the cheap and shabby signage, a substantial building lurks, and one day we decide to take a closer look. You are first to notice the date of construction – 1911 – in a grimy, ornamental little shield on a side wall before we wander around the back, into Maddern Reserve, a small, depressing public square from which we can see the back of the building, a massive brick wall covered with street art, tags and pigeon shit. You spot a graffito with the words 'RIP Junior Face Ma Nigga One Love Bro.' The square's not a welcoming space, though there have been attempts to brighten it with street art, and shifty characters are hanging around for uncertain reasons. We stay just long enough to take a few photos, then hurry back to Paisley Street.

Not much to write home about, then. But this was once the Grand.

Footscray has no cinemas today, but in the early twentieth century there were several. John Lack writes in *The History of Footscray*: 'On Saturdays the picture theatres inhaled thousands of kids at one o'clock and exhaled them again between three and four. By the early 1920s adults could go to the pictures or a dance any night of the week, excepting Sunday ... between 7 and 8 o'clock the verandah lights came on at the Barkley, the Troc[adero] and the Grand.' With theatres, dance halls, and orchestras, Footscray was a bustling entertainment precinct. The first of them all was the Grand.

The opening attracted media attention:

> The erection of large and commodious picture theatres in all the suburbs is proceeding apace, and amongst the finest of these must be reckoned the Grand Theatre in Paisley Street Footscray ... The building which is close

> to the railway station has seating accommodation for 2000 people and presents an imposing appearance. – *The Argus*, 16 November 1911.

The Grand thrived through the 1920s, but in the 1930s the Depression hit, and people no longer had the spare cash for a night at the flicks. Barely two decades after opening, the Grand closed its doors, though it was still used as a venue for public meetings, at one of which the prime minister, Joe Lyons, was hooted and booed. In 1936, writes John Lack, the theatre was reborn as the 'New Grand', splendidly fitted out with 'Glass doors, a terrazzo foyer, a marble staircase, new seating encased in vermin-resistant Dunlopillo sponge rubber ... acres of fancy plaster and a glorious golden stage curtain.' The new cinema must have been a great place for a night out. How many lovers had their first kiss in those vermin-resistant seats, while thrilling to the adventures of Errol Flynn, laughing along to Charlie Chaplin, falling in love with Clark Gable and Vivien Leigh? There were hundreds of factories in the western suburbs, but what was manufactured at the Grand was more intangible: dreams, romance, imagination.

The first Footscray cinema to open, the Grand was also the last to close. By the 1970s, it was seen as pretty archaic. The owner tried to keep it viable by reducing its size, getting rid of the foyer and the stalls. But the Grand's days ended on 8 April 1987, with the final showing of its last picture, *Heartburn*. At around the same time, in Yarraville, the Sun Theatre was also closing its doors. Shortly afterwards, the Fiesta Bingo Hall moved in, slapping its signage all over the upper storey of the former Grand. But that was never going to be a long-term solution. Bingo was already past its heyday, and this enterprise too was gone by the early 2000s. So, what is the Grand used for today?

– *Want to go to the pictures?*

The owner, a local businessman who runs the fashion store at ground level, gives us permission to go inside and have a look around. So we pass through the graffiti-covered, litter-strewn entrance and climb the staircase. There are deep fissures in the walls and the steps are stained and chipped. Like many thousands of couples before us, we enter the Grand agog with anticipation.

There's little to remind the visitor of what it used to be. The original seats have long gone; likewise, the screen. Lighting is provided by globes strung on wires. The auditorium has been repurposed as a storage place for furniture, and is packed with mirrors and vanities, armchairs and sofas, stuff with golden tassels and silver wings, more like thrones or wedding cakes than anything you'd sit on for comfort. We wander among these surreal items, and take a seat in a rococo armchair, pretending we are settling down to watch a movie. There's water damage on the ceiling, and tiny touches of art nouveau ornament on lights and ventilation ducts. High up at the back of the auditorium, we spy a small room with a door that's ajar. Balancing precariously on a vanity, I climb up and crawl in, and find myself in the projection box where the projectionist perched like the Wizard of Oz. There are still vestiges of rusty machinery, gauges and switches and dials, marked with words like 'Borders' 'Footlights' and 'House lights', and old wiring connected to what look like big toasters attached to the wall. Judging by the layout, there used to be a lot more stuff in here, but it's gone now. I poke around in the hope of finding some precious remnant of the past – perhaps an old movie poster or a reel of film – but turn up nothing except a few bits of cable and an empty coffee cup.

We wander back down the grotty stairs and out into Paisley Street, laughing as we recall our own experiences of the cinema. Doesn't everyone remember going to the movies with a significant other? When we lived in St Kilda, it was double bills at The Astor; later on, it was the Carlton Movie House; then the restored Sun Theatre in Yarraville. The most important time, though, as you remind me, was early in our relationship when we were living in Italy, near Milan, during a winter of ice and fog that gave me a permanently blocked nose. I was in a foul mood, and didn't feel like going anywhere, but you just laughed at me and made me come out to the cinema. It was *Harry, ti presento Sally* with Billy Crystal and Meg Ryan, and by the end of it I was in a good mood again and knew I was in love with the right person. Every cinema is the locus of millions of stories like that, so we wonder what stories remain of the Grand?

We find out when I post the photos on my blog. Responses pour in from people who knew and loved the theatre – memories of lolly ladies and lolly boys, projectionists and ushers, posters and candy, jaffas and fantails, *Romeo and Juliet* and *The Time Machine*. The gaps in the story are quickly filled in: the ticket box was at the bottom of the stairs, the candy bar at the top, the interior walls were covered with things like painted egg cartons – for acoustic reasons, someone suggests. People call for the cinema to be restored and reopened for occasional screenings or as an arts space. The post quickly becomes the most popular one on Melbourne Circle, which I put down to the special place cinemas hold in the community imagination. Like sporting arenas, they are places where we come together to *feel* something – joy, passion, excitement, love. That's what used to happen here, six nights a week, and that's what you lose when your suburb has no cinema. Is all that emotion embedded in the place somehow? Has it seeped into its fabric, like the rainwater staining the ceiling?

*

At the back of the Grand there's a giant paste-up on the brick wall by the street artist Baby Guerrilla. We stand together in Maddern Square and gaze, awestruck. The artwork shows a man and a woman flying through space together – or apart, depending on your point of view. These flying figures turn up on walls all over the suburbs, often down laneways, or high up where you could easily miss them. Most art tries to stop time, but Baby Guerrilla's pieces are transient. As the days and years pass, the paper peels away and the figures dissolve until eventually nothing is left – a metaphor about the passing of love, or the temporary nature of everything. One way or another, the people we love disappear. There is nothing he can do: she is slipping away, and will always be just out of reach.

DAUGHTER OF THE WEST

You fall in love again in middle age, and quite unexpectedly, with a footy team. We have lived in the western suburbs for twenty years, and have always been aware of the Western Bulldogs, the Doggies as they're generally known (or the 'Scray as old-timers call them) taking variable interest and going to occasional games, but whole seasons have passed without us noticing, too much else going on. You grew up in Sydney, and both your brothers played rugby league, so when you moved to Melbourne as a teenager, VFL was an alien culture. I never played footy, and neither did our kids. But around 2014, you suddenly become serious, and it's like a religious conversion. You are transformed into a scarf-wearing couch-yeller, a chanter in full regalia.

It's surprising to some of those who know you as a lover of nineteenth century novels, a world traveller, with annual tickets to the French Film Festival. What is this allegiance to a ratbag suburban football team? But it makes sense to me because your passion for something bigger than the individual is what I fell in love with in the first place. You've always been a sucker for an underdog, and the Bulldogs are quintessentially that, with a single premiership flag in their history, won more than sixty years ago. They're a blue-collar team in a blue-collar area, often facing disaster or even closure: the community saved the club in 1989, raising hundreds of thousands of dollars to prevent a forced merger with Fitzroy.

Your conversion has something to do with the arrival of the Bulldogs' new coach, Luke Beveridge, a man so chilled one suspects he has recently descended from a Tibetan mountain. He's the opposite of the traditional macho football coach: he speaks in parables, uses words like 'love' and 'the soul'. Interviews hint at problems with an overbearing father (and you relate to that too) but he nurtures young men rather than bullying them. We are no experts on the finer points of footy, but it's clear that the Bulldogs, under Beveridge, are keener than everyone else and work harder for each other than anyone else, hand-passing the ball at the speed of a proton in a particle accelerator. We see how much the players love him, and we love them for it. Your feeling for these boys, most of them so young and so skinny, is almost motherly. You stick up for them when opposing fans jeer. You are one-eyed in your demand for free kicks, outraged by manifest injustice. You sit on the couch knitting a red-white-and-blue scarf, shouting 'Come on Doggies! Oh, come on little Doggies! Yes! Yes! YES!' And a stitch is dropped as you punch the air.

The team is known for collective virtues, rather than individual brilliance: other clubs have preening stars, but the Dogs are a working-class outfit, and if an individual is singled out, it is always for a quality like courage and self-sacrifice. You replay on YouTube, again and again, the moment when Dale Morris, as old as God and playing with a fractured spine, cuts down Buddy Franklin (the Sydney Swans' main man) in the 2016 Grand Final, a moment that seems to epitomise the David v Goliath nature of the contest.

Their spiritual home is Whitten Oval, in West Footscray. Though AFL matches are no longer played there, it was the home of Footscray Football Club for decades. Standing out the front is the statue of former Bulldogs legend Ted Whitten, sending a booming kick over the oval named in his honour. We go there to watch training, to cheer the 'Daughters of the West' playing in the AFLW, or just to sit in the café on the off chance that St Bob Murphy, captain, half back flanker and writer, or Our Saviour Luke Beveridge might pass by. You speak to the club's community liaison officer because you want to connect the club with the African refugees in your classes. We watch the 2016 Grand Final on the big screen at the Whitten Oval, among thousands of other fans, and being there lends the place a special magic, our voices adding to the collective cheers, and at the final siren we hug each other amid the general delirium.

Is it the place that has had this effect on you? Have you inhaled the spores of allegiance in the air? Your eyes are attuned to Bulldogs iconography in the neighbourhood: a fence in team colours, the words GO DOGS painted on a wall. You never fail to point out the Bulldog-themed house on Hyde Street, the garden draped with drooping flags and rain-streaked banners, teddy bears and slogans, the windows plastered with faded pictures of past players. After the premiership win, painted bulldogs grin from the walls of local shops and the team colours are all over the inner western suburbs: everything is red-white-and-blue, even the pub. An astronaut circling the earth could recognise our neighbourhood from space. It's a kind of folk art inspired by local loyalty and sheer joy.

That great victory happened a few years ago, so most of the banners have come down, and the pub has been repainted. But traces of red-white-and-blue and GO DOGS linger. Now when I see the team colours, they remind me not of the Bulldogs, but of you.

PREMIERS
2016
CONWAY

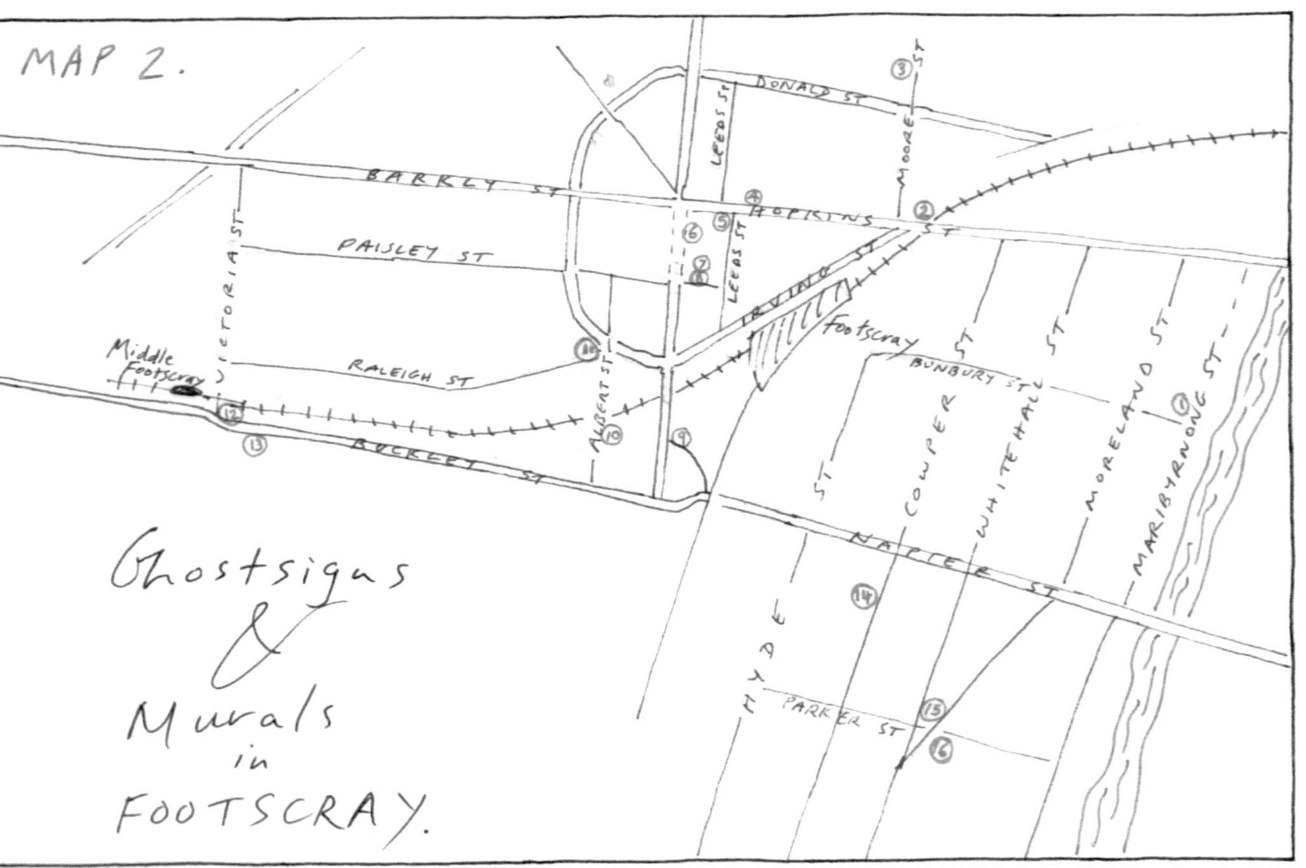
MAP 2.
DONALD ST
MOORE ST
LEEDS ST
BARKLY ST
HOPKINS ST
PAISLEY ST
VICTORIA ST
RALEIGH ST
ALBERT ST
IRVING ST
Footscray
Middle Footscray
BUCKLEY ST
BUNBURY ST
COWPER ST
WHITEHALL ST
MORELAND ST
MARIBYRNONG ST
NAPIER ST
HYDE ST
PARKER ST
1
2
3
4
5
6
7
8
9
10
11
12
13
14
15
16
Ghostsigns & Murals in FOOTSCRAY.

MAP 2.
GHOST SIGNS AND MURALS IN FOOTSCRAY

(1) Beside the river, a small building bears layers of mid-twentieth century ghost signs: 'Griffiths & Baird' (toolmakers), and 'Moloney & Watts' (engineers).

(2) A mural to Footscray icon, furniture salesman Franco Cozzo, on the wall of his shop.

(3) The vernacular signage of Moore Street milk bar.

(4) The Footscray Monte de Piete, a Victorian pawn shop, high on Hopkins Street.

(5) The Trocadero arcade once housed a cinema: a sole flower shop survives within.

(6) A ghost sign for Kidds hardware store is one of several in Nicholson Street mall.

(7) The Grand Theatre is well concealed behind signage for Fiesta Bingo ...

(8) ... an artwork by Baby Guerrilla is weathering on the back wall.

(9) In Mechanics Way, the old logo of Post Office Communications on the former Footscray telephone exchange.

(10) A mural of Malcolm Fraser, supporter of multiculturalism, painted when the Asylum Seeker Resource Centre was located here.

(11) 42A Albert Street was originally a dispensary operated in the early twentieth century by friendly societies, whose advertising is still prominent. Much later it became the Dancing Dog café.

(12) A ghostsign for Cinzano.

(13) A television and video repair shop, covered in a gallery of ghost signage.

(14) An old grocer's shop converted to apartments at 92 Cowper Street. Ghost signs of a brand of tea are at the front, and on the side wall (now obscured by trees) there are ghost signs of McAlpin's malto-pepsin self-raising flour and Preservene Soap.

(15) The former Thomas Chemicals plant is now apartments.

(16) The Docklands Cotton Mills plant houses small businesses and arts studios.

GHOST SIGNS

A basic rule of psychojogging: you see more when you look up.

We catch sight of them out of the corners of our eyes, at the second-storey level of a suburban wall. I say 'we', but with your better vision, you usually see them first. We're in Kensington. The building on the corner is an ordinary shop in a typical Victorian strip. At ground level, a new café with bright hip signage is going about its business, but up above, easy to miss, lettering in faded paint adorns the bricks. Ghost signs.

Immediately hooked, we stop to stare. Some letters suggest an unfinished crossword: -URE, -OAP, -ELL, DRA-, ELEC-. The only word that can be read with certainty is VELVET in purple capitals, curving elegantly around a window, a tribute to the ingenuity of the signwriter.

In the course of our walk, we spot hundreds, perhaps thousands, of ghost signs. Once we start to notice them, we see them everywhere, but especially around the older inner suburbs like Collingwood, Fitzroy, Abbotsford, and Kensington. Though made of paint and bricks, they are hardly physical objects at all: they are as intangible as memories or dreams. They spruik names familiar yet strange: the Melbourne Steamship Company, Ecks lemonade, Robur Tea, Greys cigarettes, Wertheim sewing machines, Monopole Cigars, Dainty Maid custard powder, Champion Footwear, Swallow and Ariell biscuits, Younghusband Wool Store, Preservene Soap, Perdriau Tyres, James Flood limousines. Sometimes there's a whole phrase: *Say Marchants please! Greys is great. No toil, only boil. Newmans has removed. A flick and they're gone!* Other times, only a few letters survive to tease the mind and the eye.

Ghost signs are beautiful and mysterious in themselves, as well as evocative windows into social and industrial history. The signage on the Younghusband warehouses reminds us that for years Kensington was a centre for tallow, hides and wool. Around Abbotsford and Clifton Hill, ghost signs summon up the footwear industry that once dominated the area. A former grocer's shop in

Cowper Street, Footscray, bears advertising for McAlpin's flour and Preservene soap on its bluestone walls. Not far from our house, there's a bright ghost sign for the old morning newspaper, *The Sun,* while beside Seddon station, you can still see signage for the former evening paper, *The Herald.* Near Flinders Street, a sign on the rear wall of a pub advertises drinking hours until 6.00 pm. (The legislation mandating this closing time, and responsible for the famous 'six o'clock swill', was abolished in 1966.) Near Elizabeth Street, a ghost sign still provides the address of 'stuff-cutters' – the trade that cut leather to size for boots and shoes. At every step, if we open our eyes, we can be alerted to the stories that populate the streets we walk in.

Sometimes they appear, or reappear, out of nowhere. A building is demolished, revealing a ghost sign on the wall next door. The apparition remains for a few months, before being obscured by whatever comes next. Sometimes they disappear overnight. A wall in Yarraville used to display a beautifully painted sign for Ecks lemonade, the only such sign I know of for this lost product, but without warning it was obliterated by a layer of black paint. Others vanish when taggers go to work. But many survive, whether by design or neglect. Some walls are layered in signs painted at different times, like *pentimenti.* On the milk bar wall in Seddon, the word 'TEA' appears next to the word 'HERALD'. Which came first? The process of weathering has brought them to light together, aptly enough: why not have a cup of tea with the evening paper? A small building beside the Maribyrnong river in Footscray reveals the names of Griffith & Baird (from the 1950s) and, more faintly,

Moloney & Watts (the 1930s). In this way, ghost signs bid us to hold different eras in our minds simultaneously.

Often, it's enough to appreciate a ghost sign simply for what it is – a discreet allusion to the past – without further investigation; at other times, we want to know more. Thanks to the internet, we can usually discover something of its heritage. A few clicks, and we know the basic facts about the Melbourne Steamship Company. But many ghost signs have faded away almost to nothing, leaving only a few stray letters to tease the eye, presenting a challenge to find out more. Even when the sign is complete, the story is not, and that is what makes them appealing to us. We love the gap that opens up for the imagination between the known and the unknown.

I zoom in with my camera on the Kensington signs. Gradually they come into focus: at least three ... two beside each other, another superimposed. The words appear as faint as breath on a window: 'Draper' can still be made out, and a name – is it Mitchell? – in white. But the two clearest signs are old brand names: Pure Velvet Soap and Electrine Candles. What were these products? On the day the signwriter climbed his ladder on a Kensington corner, passers-by would have recognised them instantly, and while we might still find Velvet soap lurking on supermarket shelves, Electrine Candles are unknown, their name archaic.

*

Once again, local history comes to our aid. Velvet Soap and Electrine Candles were both made by the same firm: Kitchen & Sons, a large Melbourne manufacturer operating from the Victorian era to the mid-twentieth century. The business of Kitchen & Sons involved boiling down animal carcases for tallow, from which soap and candles were made. This was one of the 'noxious industries' that the western suburbs were notorious for. Tallow candles were cheaper than wax ones, but created a stink when burned. Once, every working-class home in Melbourne would have reeked of tallow; but when electric light became widely available, the demand declined. Wax candles became an upmarket option, an accompaniment to romantic dinners, a decorative feature rather than a practical light source.

Given the actual source of the products, advertising campaigns were necessary to create the story behind the brand, as we say these days. Fortunately, Kitchen & Sons had an innovative publicity department, and in the 1920s they commissioned Melbourne artist Ada Outhwaite Rentoul, famous for her bestselling illustrations of fairies, to illustrate a promotional version of the book *Cinderella*, in which the good fairy advised Cinderella to use none but Kitchen & Sons products. The State Library of Victoria has a copy of the book. We call it up from the stack, turn the pages, and imagine a child reading it.

To wash your linen lily white
You should choose pure Velvet brand!

No mention there of boiling down animal carcasses: this product came straight from fairyland.

Now we want to hold an Electrine candle in our hands. We want to feel the consistency of the tallow, smell the smoke, watch it burn. We want it to light up the past for us. Does some old house have a forgotten stock of Electrine candles in the back of a cupboard or under a floorboard? Does the name have any meaning any more, or has it been snuffed out?

*

What is the significance of a ghost sign? I say it is a symbol of mortality, reminding us that everything solid is bound to disappear. You say no, it represents survival. These signs were meant to be transitory, but here they are, one hundred years later, proclaiming their message. Ghost signs are living paradoxes, presences that point to absences. Once a sign gradually fades into illegibility, or is hidden from sight, it ceases to be a sign of any kind. There is no protection for the vast majority of them: any day a familiar ghost sign might be gone, painted or bricked over or otherwise defaced. But even that is not the end of it. Images can be saved and duplicated online, and reproduced in the minds of those who saw them. They become a part of countless memories, a ghost of a ghost.

Should we think of them as the city's memories and dreams, its nightmares and desires? As we walk the suburbs, we sense presences in ruined buildings and brick walls, and feel the vibrations of past lives. We see ghosts everywhere. The city sheds its familiarity and becomes a place of weirdness and wonder, hinting at its secrets, revealing a little, but no more. Proust referred to memory as 'the inner book of unknown signs'; these signs, bright or faded, are the memories of the city.

PURE
VELVET
SOAP

THE MONKEY JOCKEYS OF WHITE CITY

I heard about White City from the writer and historian Tony Birch. 'A greyhound track out Sunshine way, gone now. It used to be very popular.' Tony pulled up a website called 'Melbourne 1945', which shows aerial photos of Melbourne in 1945, and allows the viewer to compare the city then with aerial views of the same places today. We squinted at the screen together as he scrolled over black-and-white images of the western suburbs, zooming in on Sunshine Road, which begins just south of the footy oval in West Footscray and heads west alongside the railway line towards Sunshine, via Tottenham. Back then, there were not many houses out that way, and few factories. Just the road, paddocks, and a couple of quarries. A railway line, and a single tiny platform in the middle of nowhere. And south of that, a faint white oval etched into the earth. '*That's* the dog track,' Tony said triumphantly.

*

So one hot day, you and I set out on a quest for White City. Starting at Whitten Oval, we walk from West Footscray along Sunshine Road, our eyes and ears alert for clues about the past, accompanied by the whoomp-whoomp of passing cars whose drivers throw odd glances at the strange sight of a couple on foot. Despite its name, there is nothing pretty about Sunshine Road. These days it's a place of factories (mostly closed), 'For Lease' signs, bus depots, smash repairers and container yards. It's also a site of industrial archaeology. James Flood, a maker and restorer of vintage cars, once had its premises here, and a beautiful rendering of an early twentieth-century car still adorns the walls. Imperial Chemicals (better known as ICI) was here, along with Goldsbrough Mort. Once a mighty agribusiness whose wool stores were a commanding presence throughout Australia, its Sunshine Road premises have been converted into a storage place. The former Uncle Tobys factory, maker of billions of breakfasts, has new occupants, despite the sign 'CREAMOTA' peeping from one of the chimneys, like the ghost of porridge past.

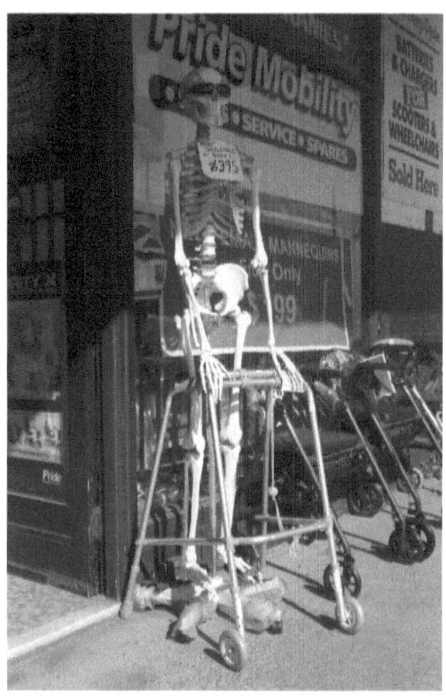

We reach the big new Tottenham station and the odd little collection of shops that huddle in the shadow of the overpass: a tattooist's, a hairdresser, a junk shop selling an eclectic offering that includes second-hand electric scooters, nude mannequins and a skeleton sporting shades – perhaps a refugee from a university's medical department. Above the shops, on one of the pediments, you spot a sign reading 'Hansen for Houses', dated 1947. Intrigued by the promise of the sign, you will later go to the Footscray Historical Society and ask about Hansen, discovering that he was a prolific builder and a key figure in post-war development: many locals are living in Hansen's houses to this day.

When we reach the site between Olympia Street and Quarry Road, we find not a dog track, but the Olex cable-making factory. A plaque on the wall informs us that the factory was opened by 'Prime Minister the Rt Hon Robert Menzies CH QC MP' on 4 April 1960. That was the era when the suburban fringe was opened up for industrial development, during a time of economic optimism. People living in Hansen's houses would have come to this factory (and to ICI, Goldsbrough Mort, and Uncle Tobys) to find work. It's on the verge of closure now.

I don't know what we think we might find as we wander around the perimeter, picking our way between piles of trash (abandoned mattresses, pallets, the usual crap you find in suburban edgelands) and peeking through fences, but all evidence of the dog track has long gone. Today, anyone who wants to know about White City can research a few facts via old newspapers and history societies, but it can only be revisited in the imagination.

*

The name White City originated in London, where greyhound racing using mechanical hares (instead of live ones as in the bloody sport of coursing) was all the rage in the 1920s. Copycat White Cities sprang up in Manchester, Glasgow, Cardiff, and even Tasmania. The new technology was in use at Sydney's Glebe Circuit, where it attracted huge crowds. In the west of Melbourne, a group of entrepreneurs saw an opportunity to provide cheap entertainment for the working classes, and in 1927 the Victorian Mechanical Hare Association set up a greyhound racing stadium on a patch of empty land on Sunshine Road, mid-way between Tottenham and Sunshine stations.

There wasn't much activity along Sunshine Road in those days, but several quarries were close by and the abattoirs and factories of

Footscray and Sunshine not far away. Greyhound racing has always been a working-class sport: while thoroughbred horses change hands for millions, ordinary people gain just as much pleasure from training or watching a racing dog, but at a fraction of the cost. Besides that, they could bet small sums at the dog track, and didn't have to get dressed up. It looked like the shareholders in White City had backed a winner, especially when the first meeting attracted 8,000 punters, along with forty bookmakers. The shareholders were elated. What could possibly go wrong?

Certainly no one expected that White City would be the target of political intervention. The state government, however, claimed that the lower classes must be protected from the morally reprehensible pursuit of betting on greyhounds. Acting with astonishing speed, the Attorney-General, Mr Bill Slater, introduced a Bill on 6 December 1927 to ban what they referred to as 'mechanical coursing'. During debate, Sir William McPherson MP complained that 'the greater portion of the persons who attend these meetings are boys and girls who are able to make bets as low as two shillings. Surely we do not want to encourage such a class of entertainment.' Sir William also referred to 'degrading and revolting scenes' and claimed that 'anyone who does not support a Bill of this kind is not standing up for the morals of the community'.

The aspect that most alarmed the gentlemen of the house was that women seemed to like it. Mr Burnett Gray MP offered this observation: 'Only a few days ago I had a conversation with a friend ... He is a great sporting man, and he took the opportunity while in London to attend a tin-hare coursing meeting. He told me there was a crowd there of 72,000 people. There were 500 bookmakers. The din was something awful. ... The vast majority of the people present were women. Many women had young children trailing at their skirts, and some had babies at their breasts. He watched these women put their one or two shillings on the dogs. He told me that he thought it was a dreadful thing.'

> *– Typical! Women aren't supposed to enjoy themselves. Those old farts in parliament. It's not much better these days ... at least we've got the AFLW.*

But what did the honourable gentlemen really have against the working people's sport? In truth, the legislation was all about defending the interests of the horse racing fraternity. Mr Richard Toutcher MP, member for Stawell and Ararat, pointed out that 'there is a very strong and monopolistic [horse] racing man in this community, who ... has influence which he has exercised to a very alarming and considerable degree.' His words were unheeded, and the Bill duly passed. Tin-hare coursing was banned because it might lure gamblers away from horse racing.

Without mechanical hares, White City had lost its biggest attraction, and the passing of the Bill bankrupted the shareholders of White City. That might have been the end of it until a white knight named Fred Watkins stepped in. Fred was an entrepreneur with a touch of P.T. Barnum about him, and he dreamed up a range of novelties to entice the punters back. He brought in live hares instead of tin hares, and held not just greyhound races but whippet races, goat races, professional foot races, and most bizarrely, greyhounds with monkey jockeys.

Wait a second ... monkey jockeys? I had my doubts the first time I heard about it, too. It sounds like an urban legend, far too silly and cruel to be true. But true it is: capuchin monkeys can be trained to cling to the sinuous backs of greyhounds travelling at 70 kph. Even in the 1930s, that was seen as a bit outrageous: the Victorian Society for the Protection of Animals condemned the use of monkeys (no one seems to have been too concerned about the welfare of the dogs) but the stunt successfully generated publicity. Melbourne newspaper *The Argus* gave two monkeys named 'Pike' and 'Badger' a run on page 3 on 11 May 1938.

MONKEYS RIDE GREYHOUNDS

Cries of "Come on, Pike!", "Ride him out, Badger!" may soon be heard at White City. For those are the names given to two monkeys which are being trained as jockeys to ride greyhounds in races. Mr. Ronald Davies is the trainer. The monkeys will show their versatility in the saddle by riding in both hurdle and flat events. Top.—"Pike" sending his mount over an obstacle yesterday. Lower.—Last-minute instructions to dog and rider.

With Fred Watkins in charge, Tottenham White City was a popular attraction from the 1930s to the 1950s. There were three meetings a week, with total weekly attendances around nine thousand. That's a good turnout: about the same number of people watched the AFL's 2016 Grand Final on a big screen at the Whitten Oval. When their dog crossed the finish line, did the White City fans cheer as loudly as we cheered our Dogs at the end of that Grand Final? Elsewhere in Melbourne, though, most people would not have known that the track existed: the west was (and still is) a foreign land.

The track wasn't just a place of entertainment in those days though: during the Depression, thousands of working-class families reared and raced greyhounds, so the dogs kept many a household up and running. (Where the monkeys came from, I don't know. Was there a circuit of professional monkey jockeys travelling from race meeting to race meeting?) White City even had its own station, serviced on race days by the Dog Train. It must have been quite something to catch the Dog Train to White City for a flutter on the monkeys.

Eventually the crowds declined, and after twenty-eight years, the venue closed on 29 December 1955. In a final irony, on the first day of 1956, the Dog Races Act came into force, which lifted the ban on mechanical racing and banned coursing with live hares, completely reversing the legislation of 1927. Fred Watkins sold the track and equipment for £113,000. A couple of years later, the cable factory occupied the site, and now it awaits its next incarnation.

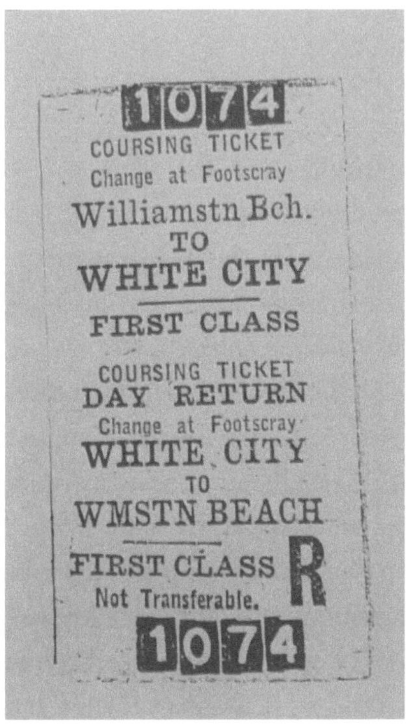

White City is silent, as if it never existed. It's preserved only in a few news clippings and photographs, and the faint memories of old-timers. There's a booklet produced by a member of a local history society, which focusses on the train and the station: that too is lost, closed in the 1980s. There are no ruins, no signs, and no official history. But maybe on a quiet night on Sunshine Road, if we listen hard enough, we might just catch the echo of a distant crowd cheering on the greyhounds and their monkey jockeys.

MODERNISM AND PEANUT BUTTER

After a browse among the mannequins and the scooters, we leave Tottenham behind us and head north up Ashley Street into Braybrook. Prayer flags are fluttering outside the Buddhist temple near Tottenham station. We pause outside for a few minutes, listening as bells chime softly while male and female voices answer each other in chants. We smile, and trying to retain a sense of peace, we continue into a streetscape less ethereal, comprising warehouses, storage places, supermarkets and smash repair shops. There's a shopping centre on the site of the wartime RAAF base, with a small model plane at the entrance. Street names around here evoke World War II: Monash Street, Churchill Avenue, Air Force Avenue, Action Street and Liberator Lane. We wend our way through quiet residential estates of brick houses, their gardens adorned here and there with Buddhas and elaborate hedge sculptures of kangaroos, and I'm reminded of a line from J.G. Ballard: 'In the suburbs you find uncentred lives ... so that people have more freedom to explore their own imaginations, their own obsessions.'

We cross the oval, where a mob of galahs is making a racket. Eventually, we arrive at Ballarat Road, where we find a building with a long, low rectangular facade, hundreds of square glass windows and a white metal frame. It looks pretty shiny and new, and if you'd never seen it before you might suppose it a new addition to the streetscape. The actual story is a bit more complicated.

We drove past the derelict shell of this building many times in the 1990s and had no idea of its history. It was a dinosaur in more ways than one: huge, skeletal, a vestige of an era that was already over. It wasn't the only one. Derelict mills and factories are scattered across the western suburbs like the temples of a lost civilisation. But this one – the ETA peanut butter factory – was different. In its day it was a celebrated piece of architecture. Today, it looks better than it used to, but much of it has been demolished, and nothing is manufactured there now except biceps and abs. When we wander through the doors, we find ourselves surrounded by smart gym equipment and serious sweaty people in active wear. On the site where workers once performed repetitive tasks on production lines, people pay to pump weights and stride on walking machines.

The building's architect, Frederick Romberg, was born in 1913 and grew up in Berlin, leaving Germany in 1933 when his leftist sympathies brought him to the attention of the Nazis. He studied architecture in Zurich and travelled to Australia in 1938, quickly finding work in Melbourne. (He was one of a number of significant European architects who came to Melbourne as refugees around the time of World War II). Local architects were impressed by the fact that he'd worked with European masters such as Gropius and Le Corbusier. One of his early projects, working with Mary Turner Shaw, was designing the stylish Newburn apartments on Queens Road, South Melbourne (constructed in 1939), followed by the much larger Stanhill apartments completed in 1950 and also on Queens Road. Both of these are still standing today, still occupied, and intact, which is more than you can say for the ETA factory.

In 1953, Romberg went into partnership with architects Roy Grounds and Robin Boyd. The famous firm known as 'Gromboyd' benefited from the economic optimism of the time and investment in manufacturing. This was around the time that Olex built its factory on the old greyhound track in Tottenham, and when thousands of homes, including ours, were built to accommodate the booming working-class population whose taste in domestic architecture was denounced by Robin Boyd in his classic work of cultural criticism, *The Australian Ugliness*. The kind of thing that Boyd hated was 'featurism', which he described as 'the concentration on frills and surface effects' – such as hedges trimmed into the shape of a kangaroo, perhaps. While Romberg was a partner in Gromboyd, the firm designed three factories, including the ETA peanut butter factory, on which he took the lead.

ETA peanut butter was already a famous name, as numerous ghost signs indicate: we have seen old ETA advertisements across the western suburbs and even as far north as Mildura. In the 1960s, ETA moved from its small factory in South Melbourne to bigger and more up-to-date premises in Braybrook. Romberg spent many hours in ETA facilities watching how they worked, and his subsequent design for the new factory was in the style that you'd expect from a follower of the Bauhaus: rectangular, like a Mondrian painting, with a long glass wall along Ballarat Road. The facade had an aluminium frame with steel columns, windows with bands of black and clear glass, and diagonal gold braces forming arrows that pointed towards the huge red letters 'ETA'. This was the administration block. The factory itself was behind it, where the serious business of peanut butter making occurred (other product lines included potato chips and chocolate covered almonds). The two structures were separated by a landscaped garden with a sculpted fountain by Teisutis Zikaras. The factory was opened by the premier, Henry Bolte in 1962. It was the only Australian building listed in an international publication of the world's best architecture that year, which no doubt further boosted Gromboyd's reputation as flagbearers of modernism in Australia.

Locally, though, ETA was famous for something else: elaborate Christmas decorations and lights, which drew big crowds. 'It was as spectacular and glamorous an event as my western suburbs childhood remembers,' according to writer Kerrie Soraghan. When I posted a story about the factory on the blog, this is what local people remembered. Community members were less impressed by the factory's pure modernist lines than the fact that Santa landed on the roof at Christmas time. At such moments, it became unexpectedly magical. 'After spending four hours travelling down in the back of our family station wagon on Christmas Eve, scouring the night sky for Santa & the reindeers, we were rewarded with the Christmas display at the ETA factory,' a correspondent wrote. (More recently, we used to do a similar thing ourselves at Christmas, driving around the streets of our neighbourhood with our daughters, looking for the houses with the most joyously over-the-top decorations.)

ETA was an important local employer. Among its thoroughly modern features were a photocopying room, a Gestetner duplicating machine, and a reception area with a plug-and-cord switchboard. An employee who started as an office junior remembered ETA as an enlightened workplace: 'The building itself had every facility staff would require. Upstairs a huge staff room with a complete kitchen where meals were cooked every day ... soup, meal and sweets. We also had morning tea and afternoon tea provided in the same room. We were discouraged from using the carpeted reception stairs, these were for visitors. The factory was very clean and well organised ... It was a great place to work and being young and foolish I left for greener pastures – never found one.'

I'm not sure exactly when the factory ceased to operate: presumably some time in the 1980s or 90s, along with so many others, when the manufacturing boom petered out. Certainly, by the early 2000s it had fallen into disrepair. In 2004, Heritage Victoria permitted partial demolition and conversion of the site into a car dealership. When the site was sold on, Heritage Victoria issued another permit that required restoration of the glass wall and front office. The developer used some of the original aluminium frame and replaced other materials, including the glass, to match the original. What's left today is a hybrid – part original and part re-creation. The gold braces and the big red letters reading ETA – perhaps the most striking of its features – are gone. The reconstructed building is smaller, but does provide a faint echo of the original. On the day we walk past, there is an unfortunate promotional balloon on top of the building, adorning Romberg's masterpiece like a clown's nose in a manner that would cause Robin Boyd, the great enemy of public advertising, to spin at high speed in his functional modernist grave.

Romberg, who died in 1992, is recognised for 'the pursuit of an Australian architecture within an international framework'. Traces of his work survive here, at a gym on Ballarat Road, for those who want to sense the distant echoes of post-war optimism and the modernist style.

And ETA peanut butter? These days it's made in China.

APOCALYPSE HEIGHTS

Psychojogging is about more than history: it's about emotions, sensations, and the curious feelings that a place can evoke in us. Some suburbs plunge us back into the past, others look forward to the future, and some seem to hover in a strange, other worldly non-time, as if we have passed through a trick mirror into an alternative reality. Such a place is Avondale Heights in Melbourne's north west. It's hard to get a handle on a suburb where there are no people in the streets, and the houses seem fine but uninhabited: there's no one in the well-tended gardens and the parks are desolate. It's as if some obscure disaster has unfolded, yet we don't know what. It makes us profoundly uneasy and triggers surreal dystopian fantasies.

*

Something happened in Apocalypse Heights.

A war, plague or tsunami. Or perhaps an explosion that killed the populace, but left the buildings standing. Or perhaps aliens took everyone to a remote planet.

Because some time between 2011, when the census was conducted, and today, 10,990 people were spirited away.

There must be some explanation. Because there's no one here. No one visible, anyway.

Not in the streets. Not in the parks. Not resting in the shade of the reserves. No kids swing on the monkey bars. No old folk play bocce. No teenagers skateboard. No one walks their dog along the Monte Carlo reserve.

There's a community centre, but no community.

A couple of dogs are barking behind fences. And is that the distant buzz of a leaf blower? A man commanding nature to withdraw? It's an illusion. There's no one.

What about that roar overhead? A plane, on the flight path to Tulla.

Cars ... yes, plenty of those. Those hunched figures behind the wheels must be survivors of the apocalypse, sealed in radioactivity-free pods. As we walk north up Military Road, the traffic is a constant swoosh and thump, swoosh and thump. Drivers, intent on getting somewhere, yack into hands-free mobiles, and follow instructions from their GPS. 'At the next intersection, accelerate and keep on going.'

But we are on foot, hacking up the street like vagabonds. Other pedestrians eye us warily. Their eyes say no one has a good reason to be on foot. Not here, not now. They are ashamed of their pedestrian status, but there is no feeling of fellowship, nor do we form a happy band of wandering brethren. Instead their glances say, *What are you up to? Where are you going? Why aren't you in your pod?* If a car hit us, it would keep going. We'd be left for carrion. Or for a passing garbage crew to toss our rotting corpses into the truck.

Spooked by Military Road, we take a right into one of the new estates. In the still heat of Sunday, we walk along Templewood Grove. Big houses. Huge. Two, three storeys. Double garages. Columns, pillars, colonnades. High pointed railings. Balconies, statues, pencil pines. And well-tended gardens. Tended by one of the abductees, presumably (or alien replicants). Well-mown lawns. And the topiary! Never have we seen so many bushes trimmed into pleasing shapes. Does Apocalypse Heights have Australia's highest population of topiarists?

Are these finely-honed shapes signals to the aliens, or communications towers cunningly concealed? Are those bushes watching us, recording our every move?

Who lives in places like this? No untidiness is permitted, nor any of the rambunctiousness of actual life. We have landed in a theme park: Apocalypse World. Dazed, we wander among the pines, the topiary, the columns, the perfect lawns. We see no one, hear no one. And gradually, our brains slowly begin to shut down. Our tongues thicken and loll. Our eyes glaze. Our feet slow, and our legs become weak.

– *We have to get out...*

I find you at an estate agent's billboard in front of a huge house. You point wordlessly. 'Unfortunately the owners have been forced to sell their dream home, which has become too large for them. It contains 6 bedrooms and 4 bathrooms. Every room is palatial. But it won't be on the market for long.'

Is that the answer? Some family has lost itself, rattling around the palatial rooms, everyone in their own bathroom. Between the plasma and the pines, a family has lost its soul. Maybe that's when the aliens came in their pod-like spacecraft, communicating through those sculpted bushes. That's when they spirited them up, the denizens of this suburb, and took them to a distant planet*, to siphon off their DNA for advanced galactic technology. Leaving behind lifeless husks. Empty streets.

And topiary.

* One notable inhabitant of Avondale Heights, according to Wikipedia, was pilot Frederick Valentich, who really was abducted by aliens. Maybe.

BOMBS ON THE MARIBYRNONG

Fleeing the alien landscapes of Apocalypse Heights, we head east towards a region in some ways even stranger. This is a place whose history lingers in its bones, though we wouldn't immediately know, just by looking at it.

It's a hot day in November. There are few people around. We approach through Steele Creek Reserve, which has been revegetated with native species by a local environmental group. To the east, there's a view of the city, some 10 kilometres distant. The reserve also has a good view across the Maribyrnong to an area of abandoned land dotted with deserted brick buildings and a chimney. But don't try to get too close: the area is fenced off, and there are scary signs forbidding trespass. Tarkovsky's film *Stalker* comes to mind: is this 'The Zone'? Nothing's going on behind the fence surrounding the deserted area, which is bordered by the river to the north, east and west, and Cordite Street to the south. Abandoned brick buildings doze in the summer heat. Glancing at each other in trepidation, and with a faint sense of dread, we creep a little closer.

The warning signs were put up by the Department of Defence. That is our only clue and there is no other information to read. There is no way in, so we will have to go away and conduct some research. Later, armed with more knowledge, we will return.

*

Defence, we find, has owned the land since 1908. Before that, the Maribyrnong racecourse and Fisher's famous racing stables were there, and before that, for thousands of years, it was the country of the Woi Wurrung people. But within more recent memory, it was a bomb factory.

We have always vaguely known that weapons manufacturing went on in the western suburbs. Friends and neighbours told us as much, and every now and then there was a story in the press about chemicals uncovered in the soil. But we've never really investigated the matter until now. The Maribyrnong site, we learn, was the site of one of the biggest explosives factories in the city, and it was during World War II that it really came into its own. Some six thousand people worked there, making cordite, nitroglycerine and TNT, which went into shells, bombs, grenades, mines, depth charges and cartridges. Hence Cordite Street. Other nearby street names hint at the history of the area: Sentry Place, Ordnance Reserve, and

Military Road, which is the main artery of Avondale Heights.

In all, according to historian John Lack, the region's munitions and ordnance factories employed twenty-two thousand people, turning out shells, mines and bullets that were proudly 'made in Maribyrnong'. Because the blokes were away fighting, the factory was a major employer of women, although their pay rate was only 90 per cent of the male rate, and after the war they were replaced by returned servicemen. Many of these women would never have worked in a factory before: it would be quite something for your first factory job to be as a bomb maker. But the wages were pretty good: over £2 a week, a lot more than a salesgirl at Myers received.

Edna Macdonald was one of the workers at the nearby Footscray ammunition factory. She recalled: 'people started to flock in, they were employing by the hundred every week and we had all types of people, sports teachers, prostitutes, you name it, they accepted anyone and it was absolutely packed to the hilt. We were making small arms – 7.2 and 9 mm – and it was horrifying for the first few weeks.'

To state the obvious, explosives factories are hazardous places. Workers had to handle sulphur dioxide and TNT, as well as sulphuric and nitric acid from cold to boiling point. Besides the inherent dangers, a simple accident could lead to the whole place blowing up. And a bomb factory was clearly a potential enemy target. Not much to smile about, one might think, going to work every day in the Pyrotechnics Annexe, yet there was a sense of camaraderie and pride amongst those working there. The Melbourne artist Sybil Craig, an official war artist, spent several months at the site painting the women at work. Her paintings (online at the Australian War Memorial website) convey a strong sense of the place and its atmosphere.

Lady Mabel Brookes, a staunch member of Melbourne's upper class, and a vigorous social organiser, was one of the more unlikely employees, albeit briefly. She worked at the factory under the name of 'Mrs Brookes', making hand grenades, and in a subsequent memoir, *Crowded Galleries*, she included an account of her experiences at the factory:

> the cutting of the explosive (in appearance rather resembling spaghetti), the neat wrapping of the silver foil and the fitting into bright cases ... a panorama of precision and order, of brass scissors and implements laid in rows ... ever-ready dust-pans and brooms to gather up a snippet of cordite in case an unguarded foot or heel generated a spark from friction ...
>
> The women were obedient to regimentation. They sat by benches and screwed in base plugs, or stood and packed and wired boxes, or filled the iron shells that fitted so comfortably into a cupped hand, and their voices and gossip went on and on unquenched ... the girls crowded around at the tea interval to ask advice: their boys had told them that they would become sterile if they worked in barratol. Would I find out? ... Abortions were discussed, the pros and cons of all types of ailments, the habits of their boys, the life story of the woman down the street, children's shoes, the movies, Leggatt's ballroom ...

The women soon discovered Lady Brookes's identity – an officer dropped her off at work in a fancy car – and they knew that she was the president of the Queen Victoria Hospital for women. They were right to be concerned about their health: TNT is easily absorbed and causes serious liver damage, and contact with nitroglycerine causes headaches and dermatitis. The factory was full of toxic dust that settled on the face and skin.

Your face clouds over at the thought of those women, and the medical consequences that must have resulted from their work:

> *– When I worked for Repat we used to help the old blokes with their health problems. But who helped these women after they finished working here?*

As we sit on the hill, looking down at the site, you tell me about your days at the Repatriation department on St Kilda Road, where you worked part-time after you left school. Your dad had made it clear that whatever your marks, there was no money for a university education, so you got yourself a job. Then the Whitlam government introduced free tertiary education, and you joyfully enrolled in an Arts degree, but continued working at Repat while you studied part-time. You described yourself as the Bored Secretary, reporting to the old codgers who ran the place. The job involved helping to provide services for returned veterans. The staff were a mixture of public service lifers, students, and disastrous drunks who somehow sobered up for a morning's work then succumbed again at lunchtime. There was a brothel next door, overlooked by the Repat offices, and when its workers took a break to sunbathe on their deck, the codgers would rush to the windows to perve. You dealt with claims for support from the vets and their families, and were as kind as you could be, though the system seemed designed to make life as hard as possible for them. Old blokes who had served their country had to write a detailed explanation justifying why they needed a new set of false teeth. A permanent public service job was a dream for many in those days, but for you it was never more than a temporary measure: what you really wanted to do was teach. Working at Repat meant you could save money for your first big trip, to Greece and Italy and France and England and Ireland, so it served its purpose in the grand plan. We walked along St Kilda Road much later on our walk: the office is now apartments and there's a bank where the brothel used to be.

After the war, the Maribyrnong factory went on providing rocket and missile components for the Australian services until 1994. The site was also used by CSIRO and Defence for research. The factory closed in 1994, and since the mid-2000s, the site has largely been vacant. Such a prime piece of real estate – with at least three kilometres of river frontage – has huge value, and real estate agents salivate over it. One tiny problem is that the site comes with built-in sulphuric acid, nitric acid, sulphur dioxide, nitroglycerine and TNT. Nevertheless, after various investigations and assessments and Master Plans and Shared Visions and the Preparation of a Remediation Action Plan, it is supposedly going to be redeveloped into a substantial residential area. If you can have a supermarket on top of an arsenic site, then why not houses on a bomb factory? According to the Maribyrnong Council website, the state government announced the decision to develop the site in April 2009. Nothing happened for a few years, then in early 2018, Defence officially put the land up for sale.

– What will they call the streets here? Sulphuric Avenue? Toxic Way?

– We're having a barbie on Hand Grenade Street.

We circle the site, heading east along Buckley Street, then turn down Afton Street into a pocket handkerchief of a suburb called Aberfeldie. There's a house open for inspection, so we wander in, climb the stairs and look out of the windows into the Zone. It feels strange to stand in the stillness and imagine the site bustling with thousands of women. The peace and quiet is a far cry from the racket and stink of the war years. But traces of the past linger below ground level. They might be out of sight, but as with the Sinking Village and the arsenic site, the land here has a longer memory than people do.

BLOOD IN THE STREETS

We have psychojogged through the suburbs of Moonee Ponds and Ascot Vale, past the Showgrounds and Flemington racecourse – still thriving today, even though many of its competitors, like the White City greyhound track, are long gone – and now we pick up our walk in Kensington. We stroll along Smithfield Road and reach the Other River, where we pause on an iron bridge. Looking west, we can see the recently built Temple of the Heavenly Queen, a Taoist temple, with a giant golden statue of the Chinese sea goddess gazing at the cranes of Webb Dock. From the bridge, we turn back towards the east, this time heading up the long bluestone path that leads towards a long-closed Melbourne icon: the Newmarket saleyards.

Typical urbanites, we are utterly distant from the reality of food production. The closest we come to farm animals is the meat counter at the supermarket and occasional visits to the Royal Melbourne Show. We took our daughters when they were little, until the price of the showbags became too outrageous, though to be fair, the animals were always impressive. Yet it's not long since millions of cattle and sheep were driven through the Melbourne suburbs on a regular basis, as they had been for more than a century. Some of the busiest stock routes ran through Kensington, and there is still plenty of evidence of them. We pause at one of the noticeboards, which displays some weathered old pictures and basic information. It tells us that Newmarket was the busiest saleyard in Australia, one of the biggest in the world, and that millions of sheep, cattle, pigs and horses were sold there at public auctions, many of them ending up as meat on the table, their carcasses boiled down for tallow.

Since the closure of the stockyards the area has been converted into residential housing, and neat new dwellings surround little areas of shared parkland. We walk on bluestone pavers along Stockman's Way, which passes under Epsom Road and up the hill to the remains of the saleyard just south of Racecourse Road. The trail is quiet and leafy, unlike its heyday, when sweating, swearing men and their dogs drove thousands of bellowing beasts along here. The racket must have been incredible, along with the occasional moments of excitement when an animal galloped off into nearby streets.

Today around the former site of the stockyards, a multitude of people are jogging, riding along the bike track, walking dogs, playing with their kids. It's tranquil and pleasant: not a raging bull to be seen. Surviving components of the saleyards include the old clock, some of the pens, and many bluestone cobbles. There's a school where the admin offices were. I must have driven past it hundreds of times without knowing what it was. We can get a good view of the saleyards from the school grounds, and spend an hour wandering among the cobbles and pens, beneath the old clock, taking photos.

When I post the photos on my blog I receive a long response from a gentleman named Edwin Day, who has detailed memories of the area and a fine turn of phrase:

> Cattle bellowing, sheep bleating, the continual banter of auctioneers cajoling the extra shilling or two from reticent buyers, or the call of spotters as they detected almost imperceivable bids. Buyers and sellers clad in gumboots and Dryzabones talked the special language

> that only stock and station men understand. A myriad of drovers, some walking and some on horseback, constantly moving the many thousands of livestock in a never ending cycle.
>
> With so many cattle and sheep being driven here, there and everywhere, it was inevitable some would stumble and break a leg, or just get down and not be able to get up again ...

When such an event happened, Edwin writes, the Dickensian figure of the 'Cockbill's man' would be sent for (turn away now if you're squeamish):

> Cockbill, resplendently dressed in suit coat, black trilby and long curled moustaches ... Removing his gold mounted briar from the pocket of his weskit, Cockbill would light up and blow clouds of smoke in the air. An examination of the stricken beast was next, after which he'd declare his intention to the assembled crowd. 'I intend to dispatch it to kingdom come.' Now came the uniform of death, each piece caked in congealed blood, a leather apron, leggings and gauntlets, a sharp knife and a bolt gun. To jeers from the crowd, Cockbill would don his uniform, steel his knife and load the gun. There'd be a resounding crack and the beast would slump motionless to the road.
>
> Next he'd pull the animal's head back and cut its throat. A huge gush of blood would spurt onto the road. The spectators would cheer their approval then promptly go home to enjoy their dinner, leaving Cockbill to load the beast onto the dray and the flies to feast on the blood in the gutter.

Associated industries sprang up in the vicinity. Along Smithfield Road, there used to be a line of slaughterhouses and wholesale butchers. Probably the animals being driven along the stock route had a rough idea of what awaited them at the end of it: 'dispatch to kingdom come', as Cockbill used to say. No wonder some tried to escape.

One of the largest pastoral companies was Younghusband & Co, a powerhouse of the wool industry. As per the ghost signs on its huge buildings on Chelmsford Street, it was famous for wool, tallow, skins, hides and fur. Tallow is animal fat rendered from carcasses, and its production involves chopping up and boiling down bits of dead animals. People in neighbouring suburbs knew which way the wind was blowing by the stink.

One of the most successful Melbourne tallow extractors was John Kitchen. He started out making candles from butchers' scraps in a South Melbourne backyard in the mid-nineteenth century, but was ordered out on the basis of it being an offensive trade. In 1870, Kitchen & Sons moved its operations to Footscray – a suburb that positively welcomed noxious trades – and went from strength to strength. Two of the firm's most successful brand names were Velvet Soap and Electrine candles – as we noted earlier, ghost signs for these products can still be seen around Melbourne. As for Younghusband & Co, when we call in on its impressive brick complex, we discover that by 2015 it has become a 'creative designer precinct', the home of independent arts organisations and niche shops. We wander among industrial relics repurposed as design features: old office equipment, signage from buses and trains, and bits of machinery that can now be acquired as nostalgic home accessories.

Maybe we needn't lament the loss of the saleyard and the noxious industries that accompanied it, but nevertheless, the presence of stock routes through the suburbs meant that city dwellers were aware of the country and its role in putting food on their table. These days, it's easy for urban types like us to imagine that meat, leather and wool – let alone soap – appear in shops by magic, and never have any conception of where they come from. The airbrushed actor-farmers who appear on supermarket advertisements are nothing like those cursing drovers who brought the beasts to market. The sources of our food are as remote to us as the makers of the clothes we wear: a cow is almost a nostalgia item. And we might not see a sheep – or a farmer – from one year's end to the next, let alone the Cockbill's man committing slaughter in the street.

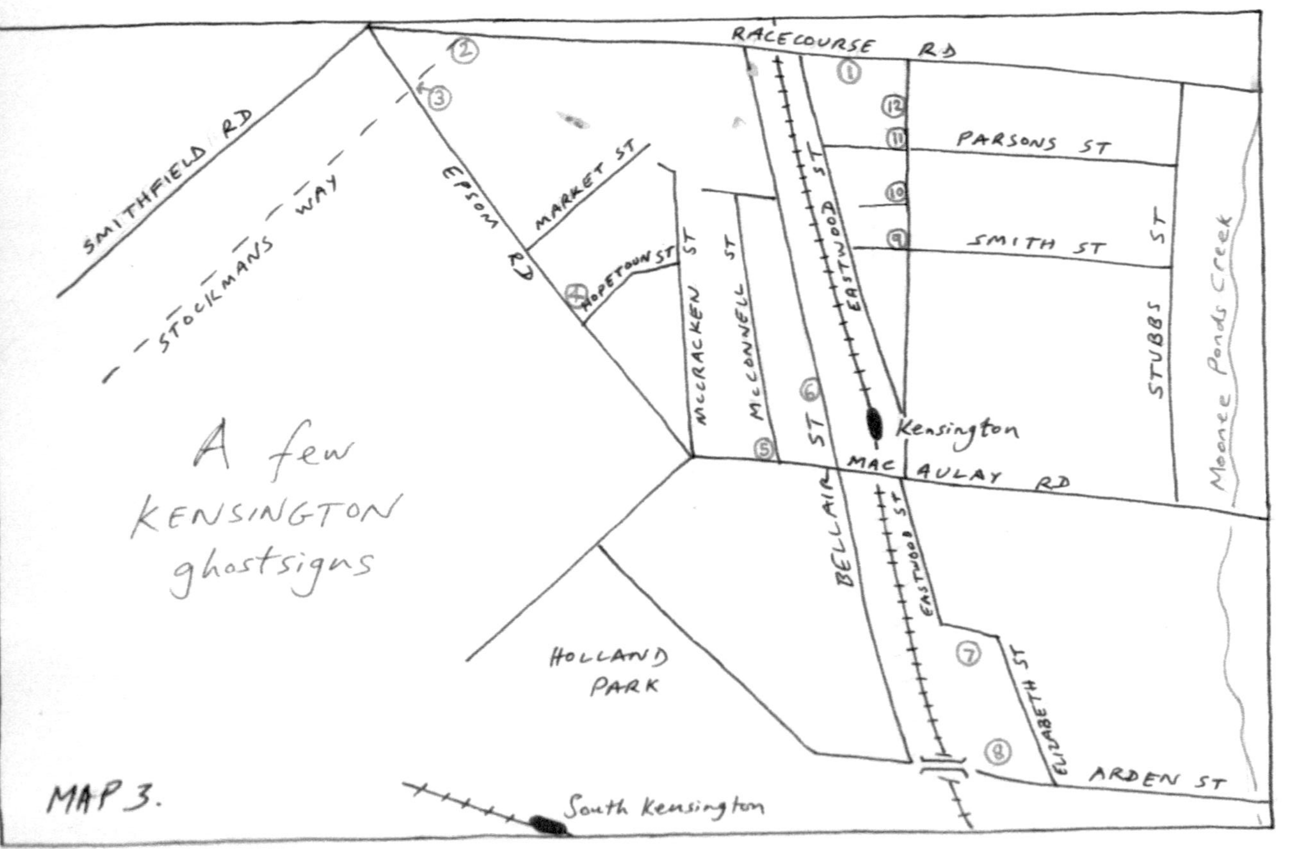

A few KENSINGTON ghostsigns
MAP 3.
RACECOURSE RD
SMITHFIELD RD
STOCKMANS WAY
EPSOM RD
MARKET ST
HOPETOUN ST
McCRACKEN ST
McCONNELL ST
BELLAIR ST
EASTWOOD ST
PARSONS ST
SMITH ST
STUBBS ST
Moonee Ponds Creek
Kensington
MAC AULAY RD
EASTWOOD ST
ELIZABETH ST
ARDEN ST
HOLLAND PARK
South Kensington
1
2
3
4
5
6
7
8
9
10
11
12

MAP 3.
A FEW KENSINGTON GHOST SIGNS

(1) On Racecourse Road, among the diverse cultures of today, ghost signs from earlier eras survive: a newsagent on a Victorian building at 309a is close to the more recent Armato Bros at 305.

(2) Near the intersection with Smithfield Road is the entrance to the former stockyards. Walk along Stockmans Way ...

(3) ... and pause to admire the mosaics under the footbridge.

(4) At 46 Epsom Road, a well preserved ghost sign: 'Orders received for Wines & Spirits ...' accompanied by 'Bran, pollard, chaff, oats' – feed for horses.

(5) At 520 Macauley Road, the corner shop with layers of ghost signs for Velvet Soap, a Draper, and Electrine Candles; on the Macaulay Road wall, 'Empire Cocoa' is very faintly visible.

(6) At 156 Bellair St., close to the station, the signage of Bill Pearce's plumber's shop, along with its old telephone number FF1666.

(7) On Elizabeth Street, two industrial landmarks: the Younghusband & Co building, marked prominently with signage for Fur, Wool, Hides, etc; a little further down, the Allied Flour Mills, originally Kimpton's, with a cute 'Self raising department' sign.

(8) A Kimpton's ghost sign is faintly visible from the railway footbridge on Arden Street.

(9) On Rankins Street, there are several ghost signs in close proximity: metal signage on the Simmie's factory ...

(10) Robur Tea ...

(11) ... Quality Butcher ...

(12) ... and another United Friendly Societies (UFS) dispensary.

THE CURIOUS CASE OF DR MORSE

We are always on the alert for ghost signs now. Once we start seeing them, we spot them everywhere. Certain names recur frequently, like familiar faces in a crowd: Robur Tea and its rival Bushells, for example, pop up all over the suburbs, testament to the 'tea wars' of the early twentieth century, when the marketing departments of Robur and Bushells were locked in a battle for market share. Others are more mysterious and elusive, and refuse to give up their meaning without some effort on our part. When we encounter one of these, we stand together, our necks craning upwards for long minutes, our lips silently moving as we try to shape the words we are reading. At 445 Abbotsford Street, North Melbourne, we find several old signs superimposed on the one wall, the newest at the top, the oldest a few layers down, faded and almost illegible.

The sign at the top right is easy: it's Penfolds Wine, whose ads appear all over the Melbourne suburbs (including a superb one for Maison Marney brandy in nearby Canning Street). This was painted more recently than, and over the top of, the ones below. Even so, it has deteriorated in recent years: photographs online show that not long ago the tagline '1844 to Evermore' appeared clearly below the brand name, but now those words are almost illegible, the 'Evermore' gone into eternity.

The sign on the lower half is more of a puzzle, as the brand itself is a ghost, absent from its own sign. Just what is being advertised here?

– Maybe Penfolds was painted over the top ...
– Yes – there's something underneath – what does it say?
– 'Wash Clothes But Will Clean Metal and Woodwork Well'
– Doesn't make sense. And what's that animal at the bottom? Is it a dog?
– A monkey, I think ....
– But why is it wearing a suit?

Later, we type the 'Wash Clothes' slogan into Trove, and come across an ad from *The Age*, 10 December 1904, for a product called Monkey Brand that uses almost exactly the same words: 'Won't wash clothes but will clean well metal & woodwork'. Apparently the word that has faded to illegibility in the ghost sign is 'Won't'. It seems odd to lead an ad with what your product *won't* do, but that's not the strangest thing here. On closer examination, we see that the animal figure is indeed a monkey wearing a suit, like a butler standing ready to clean your metal and woodwork. Are there more ghost monkeys on duty across the suburbs, almost washed away by time?

The third sign, the most enigmatic, appears top left. In white letters, as if in a partly completed crossword puzzle, we can read 'DR MOR –' and 'IND –'. At first, that's all I can see, but your eyes are sharper, and as we gaze more closely you triumphantly point out the ghostly black letters that gradually materialise in the background: an N, a large R, a T. Our patience is finally rewarded, and the words come into focus: 'Dr Morse's Indian Root Pills.'

Like Monkey Soap, Dr Morse's Indian Root Pills was not a local Melbourne brand. It was one of the most successful of the squillions of patent medicines that emerged in America in the nineteenth century, and the brand survived as recently as 1960. Indian Root Pills were supposed to cure just about everything, including dyspepsia, constipation, flatulence, scrofula, dysentery and 'female complaints'. The ubiquity of the company's advertising was referred to by Hal Porter in *The Watcher on the Cast-Iron Balcony*: 'Mile after mile of post and rail fences are lettered with injunctions to use DR MORSE'S INDIAN ROOT PILLS, FLUXITE, SHINOLEUM, SILVER STAR STARCH, WITCH SOAP (NO TOIL, ONLY BOIL), and KEEN'S MUSTARD.'

Why 'Indian Root'? In the nineteenth century, Native American knowledge of herbs and plants was regarded as a great selling point for patent medicines. The company had an advertising department worthy of *Mad Men*, and knew the importance of a powerful origin story. This material can still be found online, where one can read about Dr Morse, an American medical practitioner who completed his training by spending three years among Native Americans (or 'red men' as the advertising called them) where he learnt about traditional herbal remedies. Here's what happened – according to the company – when Dr Morse returned home to find his aged father close to death:

> A rumbling noise was heard in the distance, like a mighty chariot winding its way near, when all at once a fine span of horses, before a beautiful coach, stood before the door, out of which alighted a noble and elegant-looking man. In a moment's time he entered the room, and embraced the hand of his dear father and mother. She clasped her arms around his neck and fainted away.
>
> The Doctor, surprised to see his father so nearly gone, immediately went to his coach, taking therefrom various plants and roots, which he had learned from the Red Men of the forest as being good for all diseases, and gave them to his father, and in about two hours afterwards he was much relieved ... and now we behold him a strong, active man, and in the bloom of health, and at the age of ninety-five able to ride in one day thirty-five miles.

Mighty chariots! Fainting women! Old men raised from their deathbeds! Pretty powerful stuff. Unfortunately, it's bollocks. No such person as Dr Morse ever existed: the company invented him. Comstocks, a ruthless patent medicine firm with a long list of products, fabricated Dr Morse to ensure that the guy who actually invented the pills did not have his name anywhere near them. The story subsequently became an effective piece of advertising, and was included with every packet of pills.

So this painted sign on Abbotsford Street is a ghost pointing to a product that no longer exists, named after a man who never lived.

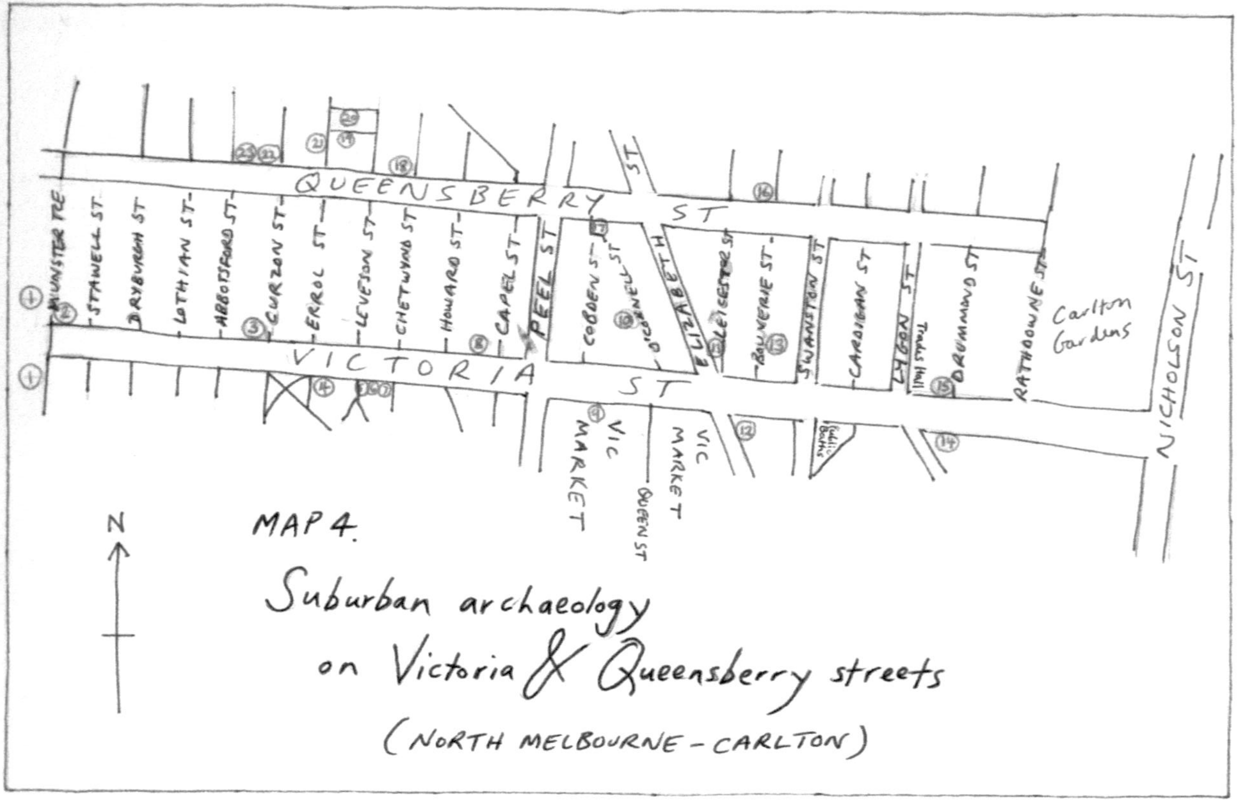

QUEENSBERRY ST
VICTORIA ST
MUNSTER TCE
STAWELL ST
DRYBURGH ST
LOTHIAN ST
ABBOTSFORD ST
CURZON ST
ERROL ST
LEVESON ST
CHETWYND ST
HOWARD ST
CAPEL ST
PEEL ST
COBDEN ST
O'CONNELL ST
ELIZABETH ST
LEICESTER ST
BOUVERIE ST
SWANSTON ST
CARDIGAN ST
LYGON ST
Trades Hall
DRUMMOND ST
RATHDOWNE ST
Carlton Gardens
NICHOLSON ST
VIC MARKET
QUEEN ST
VIC MARKET
Public Baths
N

MAP 4.

Suburban archaeology on Victoria & Queensberry streets

(NORTH MELBOURNE - CARLTON)

MAP 4.
ALONG VICTORIA STREET

(1) At the east end of Victoria Street, North Melbourne, the former Guests factory displays ghost signs, high up, reading 'Biscuits and Cakes' as well as the name T.B. Guest. It is now apartments.

(2) The former Mulcahy's Hotel with its attractive tiles is also apartments.

(3) The building with a small train atop its facade is Loco Hall, formerly the HQ of the Locomotive Engine Drivers Association.

(4) A cute little deco building at 355 Victoria Street: the numbering is particularly beautiful.

(5) A series of ghost signs: Sergio's hairdressers with its mismatched typography.

(6) *The Age* and Wertheim (famous for pianos and sewing machines), but the word below Wertheim seems impossible to decipher.

(7) Hennessy Bros, a historic bakery.

(8) On the side wall of number 354, try to decode the crossword puzzle of a ghost sign with fragments of a name and number.

(9) The old iron arcades of Victoria Market and old signage in the glass windows.

(10) On O'Connell Street, several ghost signs refer to the motor vehicle industry.

(11) The impressive Rechabites building on Elizabeth Street indicates the significance of this pro-temperance organisation.

(12) On the opposite corner, a fountain installed by the Women's Christian Temperance Union.

(13) A massive development on the site of a former bluestone brewery: old signage is visible on the Bouverie Street facade.

(14) Horti Hall – read the lovely ghost signs around the Victoria Street entrance, then crane your neck for a view of the quaint old signage on the side wall that includes meeting times of the Orchid Club and the promise of a 'Cordial welcome'.

(15) The Plumbers Union building – a classic example of Melbourne brutalism.

(16) Signage for the Melbourne Metropolitan Tramways Board, MMTB.

(17) Striking ghost signs on Cobden Street.

(18) Old signage for the Victorian Showmen's Guild.

(19) The little bluestone laneways and other small streets and alleys around Errol Street are well worth a detour. Look out for the 'Draper' ghost sign high up on Bendigo Street ...

(20) The Johnstone sign on Byron Street ...

(21) The Auction Rooms and more on Errol Street.

(22) At 590 Queensberry Street, the former signwriting shop still sports its 1980s stylings and phone number.

(23) A discreet, faded Nestlé chocolate ghost sign on the wall of no. 596.

SANDS & MCDOUGALL'S BOOK OF EVERYTHING

Like many of these stories, it begins with a ghost sign.

We have often walked and driven past the six-storey red-brick complex at 357 Spencer Street, noting its impressive presence, without ever pausing for a closer look. One day, we stop to examine the clear signage that still proudly declares the names Sands & McDougall. Beneath it are the words 'Printers and Lithographers'.

Moving closer, we notice that the names are moulded into the pediment at the top, beneath a carved figure of a rearing horse. Whoever Sands & McDougall were, their headquarters were substantial, and they were confident enough of their longevity to inscribe their names on it. This was no pop-up. (In contrast, the more recent signage tacked onto the building, like so much around Melbourne, has an unmistakably temporary feel.) Who were Sands and McDougall? We visualise two Scottish businessmen walking the streets of nineteenth century Melbourne, like characters in a costume drama. And yet now there is no company of that name. The matter calls for investigation.

Sands & McDougall was Melbourne's leading printer and publisher for well over a century, and did not close its doors until 1994. It produced vast quantities of printed material, from royal commission reports to the rules of racing: books, maps, tram tickets, banknotes, stationery, art prints, advertising, envelopes, packaging, and much more besides. The proud horse galloped across squillions of documents. Almost everyone who lived in Melbourne, or anywhere in Victoria, had the work of Sands & McDougall in their home or their pockets. By 1896, the company had separate departments for lithography, binding, ruling, sewing, gilding, colouring, photography, envelope folding, engraving, embossing, boxes, linotype, composing, and machine printing. (You can find photographs of the company's activities at the State Library of Victoria.)

But its most celebrated creation was the annual Sands & McDougall directory of Melbourne, which it produced every year from 1862 to 1974. Prior to that, from 1857–61, it was briefly known as Sands & Kenny's directory. (McDougall's predecessor, Kenny, is to the business what Pete Best was to The Beatles: there at the start but not during the years of glory.) The Sands & McDougall directories listed every householder and business in every building in every street in every suburb of Melbourne, regional cities and country towns. These millions of bits of information were laboriously gathered by a team of 'walkers' who went door-knocking to identify the occupants of every address. As walkers ourselves, we are impressed by the thought of these legions of scribes going door-to-door, patiently gathering data for the guide. It was almost as comprehensive as the census, and they did it *every year*.

The information was organised and cross-referenced in a number of ways: by street (so you could look up, for example, who lived at any address in Melbourne); by surname; and by profession and trade (so you could find your local butchers, bakers and stump-jump plough makers). The army of walkers carried out their task diligently: 'There is simply nothing to match these directories for their reliability, comprehensive coverage, and continuity of publication', writes John Lack.

Not surprisingly, given the amount of information included, the books became colossal. As the population of Melbourne grew, so did the directories, until they ran to thousands of pages, each crammed with closely-packed columns of data. Every country town in Victoria was covered, however small, including (in 1946) Kadnook, 221¼ miles from Melbourne, whose sole entry was that of R. F. Jamieson, station master. Who, we wonder, was the roving reporter who caught a train to Kadnook, took down the name of the station master and came home again?

The directories are an amazing repository of information of use to businesses, sales people, mail order companies, debt collectors and the police. These days, they are a godsend to historians, researchers, historical novelists and genealogists, not to mention wandering psychogeographers. Want to find out who lived at 25 Abbotsford Street in 1913? No problem, Sands & McDougall it! Want to know a granny's address in Collingwood in 1966, or the plumber whose name appears on a ghost sign? Sands and Mac has the answer. When we are seeking the history of Mr Vowles's Underclothing Depot in Williamstown, it is Sands & McDougall that provides the answers. The book was the Google of its day, and much of the information it contains can be found nowhere else.

Now that we know about the existence of these directories, we need to hold one in our hands. But where can we find one? The University of Melbourne's Baillieu Library has a collection of them, almost complete – I heard a story that they were recovered from a skip by an alert passing librarian when the company closed down. Anyway, there they are, a couple of walls of dense faded red, more than a century's worth, from the late nineteenth to the late twentieth centuries. We pull the massive volumes off the shelf: they make a thump on the table like a bag of cement, causing students to raise their eyes from their laptops in surprise. But when we start leafing through those pages, with their thin, thin lines of print, we become absorbed. It takes a while to figure out the system, and the abbreviations – *hrdrsr* is hairdresser of course, but what did '*Snelling, Mrs J E, cks*' mean? Ah, she made cakes! *grcr* is grocer, *tbcnst* is tobacconist, *Chas* is Charles, *Regd* is Reginald, *Clrnce* is Clarence. There's a weird kind of intimacy about looking into this book, as if we are snooping into people's lives, opening their mail or peeping through their windows. The sheer amount of information is incredible, though some of the gaps are telling: there are more than a few non-Anglo names, but sometimes the entry simply reads *Chinese* or *Italian*, as if obtaining an actual name from the occupants was too hard. The State Library of Victoria also has some Sands & McDougall directories, but not for public use: they can only be accessed on microfiche, which is tricky when you are trying to search thousands of pages. When we figure out how to navigate our way around the book, it's easier to use a hard copy – despite the strain to the wrists.

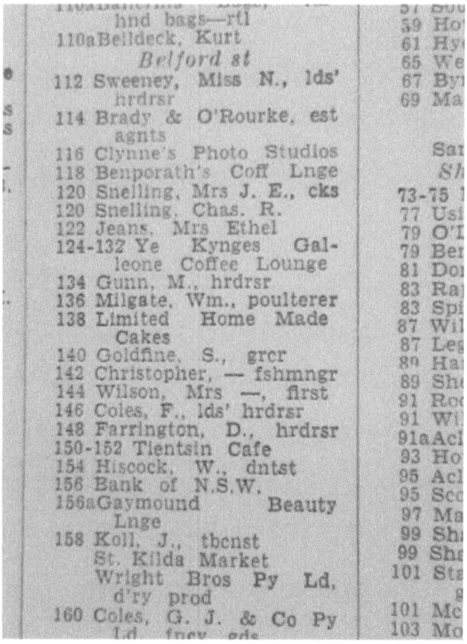

hnd bags—rtl
110aBelldeck, Kurt
Belford st
112 Sweeney, Miss N., lds' hrdrsr
114 Brady & O'Rourke, est agnts
116 Clynne's Photo Studios
118 Benporath's Coff Lnge
120 Snelling, Mrs J. E., cks
120 Snelling, Chas. R.
122 Jeans, Mrs Ethel
124-132 Ye Kynges Galleone Coffee Lounge
134 Gunn, M., hrdrsr
136 Milgate, Wm., poulterer
138 Limited Home Made Cakes
140 Goldfine, S., grcr
142 Christopher, — fshmngr
144 Wilson, Mrs —, flrst
146 Coles, F., lds' hrdrsr
148 Farrington, D., hrdrsr
150-152 Tientsin Cafe
154 Hiscock, W., dntst
156 Bank of N.S.W.
156aGaymound Beauty Lnge
158 Koll, J., tbcnst
St. Kilda Market
Wright Bros Py Ld, d'ry prod
160 Coles, G. J. & Co Py

But as our obsession grows, it's not enough to access the books in libraries – we need our own copy, at least one, if not a whole set. So many were published that one would think they must be everywhere, but it's not that easy to track them down. In the end, I locate a 1946 edition that I buy online from a man who found it under his carport during renovations. The cover is stained but the pages are in good shape. With more than 2,400 pages, it weighs about 5kg and is 12cm thick. Choose a street, walk down it in your imagination and see who was there at the time. Acland Street St Kilda, for example: hairdressers, cafes, cake shops and dentists, Ye Kynges Galleone Coffee Lounge and the Gaymound Beauty Lounge. At the top of Collins Street: physicians, surgeons, oculists and dentists, giving way to frocks and dancing schools, lingerie makers, milliners and hairdressers between Swanston and Elizabeth Streets. On Paisley Street, Footscray, near the Grand, back in the days when it was an operating cinema: Mrs Horsington's milk bar, Mrs Wilks the confectioner, a couple of solicitors, the Paisley Frock Shop, the Baptist church and the Sunday school. Our house on Hawkhurst Street isn't listed – nothing was built here until the 1950s – but the older part of Yarraville is included. Recently some old signage reappeared during renovations of a small shop on Anderson Street, and the word 'CAKES' saw the light of day briefly when the new owners replaced the fascia. We look it up: sure enough, a pastrycook (*pstryck*, as the book has it) named Hinson is listed at the address in 1946.

Turn to the trades section and one finds a record of the industries that employed Melburnians, from bootmakers and stuff-cutters (dozens of them, mostly in Clifton Hill, Abbotsford and Collingwood) to shorthand writers, private detectives, confectioners (six whole pages worth, perhaps two thousand names – far more than the number of dentists), mercers, signwriters, furriers, coachbuilders, blacksmiths, brassfounders, elocution teachers, and something called a *poundkeeper*. It's interesting what is *not* there: no childcare centres (but a few creches), no gyms, no nursing homes, no nail salons. A few physiotherapists, but no psychologists. And certainly no management consultants, web developers, or public relations firms. Lots of estate agents, though. Some things never change.

Looking for old friends, we find Cockbill the slaughterman listed as a purveyor of 'artificial manure' on Footscray Road; Sir Norman Brookes the tennis champ (husband to Lady Mabel) in Walsh Street, South Yarra; Sybil Craig the artist in a studio at 123 Collins Street; Frederick Romberg, architect of the ETA factory, in an office on Latrobe Street; White City and the Victorian Coursing Association active on Sunshine Road. The adverts in the directory promote companies, brands and attractions now forgotten: '7X – the better drink, available at all confectioners', the Melbourne Wire Works and the Metallic Bellows Co, and the Glaciarium ice rink in South Melbourne. Overall, the effect is to remind us of L.P. Hartley's observation that 'the past is another country', though it is connected to our own by wormholes in time and space.

Inevitably, production of the directory could not continue for ever. By the 1970s, the amount of work involved in criss-crossing the ever-expanding city, knocking on every single door, was too great. By then, the directory had competition in the form of free telephone directories which most households found more useful, and advertising revenue fell as advertisers turned to the mass audiences of television and radio. The directory was no longer profitable and was printed for the last time in 1974. The company continued for a few more years with its other activities before closing its doors, and a great Melbourne name ceased to exist, except for the signage on its Spencer Street premises.

One day, perhaps, all this data will be digitised and available online. But for now, we depend on hard copies. And there's something about the sheer heft of a directory that can't be replicated with the click of a mouse. Millions of copies were produced over the years, but the challenge today is to find a complete set. Thousands must have been sent to landfill, but no doubt stray copies lurk in old libraries and dusty cupboards, forgotten.

Our minds go back, past the pages of the directory, to the anonymous people who patiently gathered the information, year after year. For us, suburban strolling is a pastime, but for those professional walkers, it was a career. In fact, many of the jobs that used to involve pounding suburban streets, going door-to-door, have disappeared with the demise of travelling salespeople: in the days of Google, who would buy a set of *Children's Britannica* from a bloke knocking at the door, as my parents did in the 1970s? There are still a few people who walk for a living – census takers, charity collectors, Jehovah's Witnesses, people selling electricity plans – but even postmen tend to be on motorbikes these days. As we drift through the suburbs, we like to imagine that we are connected across time with the weary foot-soldiers of Sands & McDougall, out in all weathers, notebooks in hand, sore knuckles poised to knock on yet another door.

AN APPOINTMENT WITH DR KING

His name appeared at a construction site near the corner of Lonsdale and Russell Streets, Melbourne, in April 2013. The building on the corner had been demolished and the painted sign – hidden for many years – was exposed again, high on an adjacent wall at second storey level. Facing south down Russell Street, it proclaimed in large black capitals: 'Consult celebrated specialist Dr King, MRCS. Consultation free.'

No address, no phone number. No hint as to what kind of specialist Dr King was.

Perhaps other people wandering past that site, or standing at the pedestrian crossing waiting for the lights to change, looked up and wondered: who was Dr King?

I asked Stephen Banham, a typography expert, about the age of the typeface. He immediately picked it as late Victorian: 'The character and strength lies in the beautiful wedge serifs and the diagonal leg of the K.' This made it particularly interesting. Most ghost signs that we've seen date from the twentieth century: there are few as old as Dr King's.

The demolished Victorian building that revealed the ghost sign was a substantial four-storey structure. Originally the Tower Hotel, by 1946 (according to Sands & McDougall) it had morphed into the

Athenian Cafe, and much later on it became a Greek community centre (I remember it sporting a big 'restore the Parthenon Marbles' banner in the 1990s). The first mention of the Tower Hotel on that site is in the 1891 Sands & Mac. Dr King's sign must predate the hotel, and was perhaps obscured soon after it was painted, which is why it was preserved in such good shape.

The definitive history of Melbourne in late Victorian times is *The Rise and Fall of Marvellous Melbourne* by Graeme Davison. He describes an era of extravagance, accompanied by an orgy of building, land speculation and commercial activity which collapsed in spectacular fashion in the 1890s (a pattern repeated in the twentieth century). The city was a magnet for characters seeking their fortune, and the population almost doubled from 1880–1890, touching half a million.

Melbourne's medical world at that time was in a state of flux, poised between anarchy and reform. Practitioners included picturesque figures like the surgeon James Beaney, famous for working in a blood-stained coat, sporting diamond rings and quaffing champagne with his patients if they survived. Simultaneously, a new breed of young medical graduates emerging from the University of Melbourne were keen to introduce a more scientific, professional approach to the practice of medicine.

And then there were the 'quacks', a term used for anyone outside the medical mainstream, ranging from herbalists, homeopaths, and others who genuinely believed in alternative therapies to spiritual healers and outright con artists. The nineteenth century was a golden age of quackery in many parts of the world and Melbourne was no exception. The profession was largely unregulated, and no law prevented unqualified laymen from performing procedures, a fact much railed against by doctors' associations. But Attorney-General Alfred Deakin was unwilling to introduce legislation, preferring to let the market sort it out. As Davison puts it, Deakin was 'determined to maintain the "rights" of dissident schools of professional thought, such as homeopathy and herbalism, and the vested interests of unqualified, but indispensable, bush practitioners.' Whatever mainstream doctors thought, alternative practitioners had the right to set up practices among their more respectable fellows at the top of Collins Street, in Spring Street and near the Melbourne Hospital in Lonsdale Street.

Where did Dr King fit into this picture? Naturally, the first place to look was Sands & McDougall.

The first mention of a Dr King (no first name, no initial) under 'Physicians and medical practitioners' was in 1889, at 28 Russell Street. In 1890 he reappeared a few doors down, on the corner of Russell Street and Flinders Lane. This time there was a first name and initial: Dr James W. King. Dr King's two appearances don't suggest a long and distinguished career, in Melbourne at any rate. But he didn't lack hubris. Anyone who commissions an advertising sign that size intends to make a splash.

Melbourne and country newspapers are archived and searchable online in the National Library of Australia's online platform, Trove. And we found this 'notice' in *The Kerang Times* in March 1890:

> PUBLIC NOTICE!
>
> The Australian Medical Institute has engaged the eminent specialist Dr King, MRCS Etc as its chief medical officer. Dr King has enjoyed an exceptionally large practice as a specialist. He is a member of the Royal College of Surgeons, and legally qualified registered general practitioner in Victoria.

That sounds pretty good, if a bit self-glorifying. But the ad goes on:

> The above named institute has also succeeded in obtaining the valuable services of a highly accomplished MEDICAL CLAIRVOYANT whose power in diagnosing disease and discovering the exact state of a patient is truly wonderful. ... No questions need be asked, all that is required is a letter written by the person, or a lock of hair, neither of which must be touched by others than the one sending; this is all that is required to assure a most concise and complete diagnosis of the patient's condition. Fee for such diagnosis 10s 6d. Treatment and diagnosis £1. Call on our address Dr J King, 42 Russell St, corner of Flinders Lane, Melbourne.

By now we had serious doubts about Dr King's methods, but

if he was genuinely a Member of the Royal College of Surgeons (MRCS) then he presumably had some medical credibility. I emailed the archivist at the College in London, who replied that there was no trace of a Dr James W King in their medical register or directory for the relevant period.

That seemed to settle it. He was a quack.

*

> *– Just imagine some poor woman reading that advertisement …*

Let's call her Agnes. She's a farmer's wife in a country town. They grow oats and barley, and run a couple of horses, a few cattle. The town is doing all right: irrigation methods have been successful, and the population has grown to about a thousand. There's a new railway connection, churches, a school, a general store. Life is a struggle, but the family's not doing badly.

But she hasn't been feeling well. She's a tough country woman and doesn't make a fuss: with a bunch of little ones, and hard physical work from morning 'til night, she doesn't have time to fall ill. If she gets a headache, she just puts on tighter shoes to take her mind off it. There's no doctor in town, so nostrums from the local chemist are all she can get her hands on. She's put up with it for months. But the headaches are blinding and lasting for days, and nothing seems to help.

Then she sees an advertisement in the local newspaper. 'All that is required is a letter written by the person, or a lock of hair …' Agnes has some money put aside. She deliberates for weeks – 10/6 is not a small sum – but she's desperate. Eventually, after a day when she is almost crying from pain, she thrusts the money into an envelope along with a lock of her hair and sends it to Dr King at 42 Russell Street.

The doctor has his feet up on his desk when the letter arrives, idly wondering whether it's time to invest in a new embroidered waistcoat. It may look a little flash, but he doesn't care about that. He opens Agnes's letter, scans it, pockets the money, tosses the lock of hair into the waste-paper basket, and yells for his office boy.

'Send this creature a letter, will you?'

'Which letter?'

'Dangerous condition of the kidneys. And a price list.'

With that taken care of, he turns his mind to another question. Recently, the medical associations have been broadcasting abuse of alternative practitioners like himself all over the press, even getting in the Attorney-General's ear to have them struck off for 'imposture'. King cares nothing for the attacks on his qualifications and character – in his own mind, he's a perfectly good doctor – but the constant attacks are bad for business. He seizes pen and paper and composes a thundering riposte. When the lad slouches back in, King hands him the notice and tells him to run it down to the office of the *Record,* a newspaper in Emerald Hill, South Melbourne.

> Remember, Dr King is a qualified and registered physician, not a quack. He is a member of the Royal College of Surgeons, and duly authorised to practice as a specialist in the British provinces.
>
> DR KING warns the reader against the barefaced imposters, so called specialists etc, who, having only a money end in view, thrive on the credulity of this community by their fraudulent announcements. Dr King's reputation as a citizen, and unparalleled success as a specialist, entitles him to your confidence. Furthermore, he guarantees to cure every case undertaken. Therefore, in consulting him, patients may feel assured that they shall receive the honest advice

> of one fitted by superior skill and education, the result of an incomparable practice. – *Emerald Hill Record*, 20 December 1890.

A few weeks pass. Agnes's condition is worse. She opened her letter from the 'medical clairvoyant' with great excitement, but the brief diagnosis, which seemed to disregard her symptoms, disappointed her, especially as it was accompanied by pages of advertising and enthusiastic endorsements for Dr King's patent elixir. All the same, she sent off for a bottle, guaranteed to cure all diseases of the head, liver, heart and lungs. The elixir provides temporary relief, even a short-lived euphoria. But the headaches return, and Agnes finds herself taking larger doses for the same effect. She raids her savings and sends another letter to Dr King, earnestly craving a larger supply. And then she waits. And waits.

*

The medical world professionalised itself to some extent during the 1880s. The Medical Society of Victoria, run by a clique of venerable old-timers, was challenged by the British Medical Association (Victorian branch) which attracted younger, local graduates. The BMA fought for the establishment of a medical council to regulate the profession and kick out any doctor guilty of 'infamous conduct'. They argued that this would benefit the public by protecting them from quacks, but the counter-argument prevailed. Many of the general public supported 'irregular' practitioners, who were sometimes their only option, especially in rural areas. (Doctors would not gain the right to exclude practitioners for 'infamous conduct' until 1933.) The public debate around these issues must have at least raised public awareness about quack doctors, if it did nothing to rein them in.

Dr King wasn't the only 'medical clairvoyant' in town: this

was a popular therapy in the late nineteenth century. Related to spiritualism, medical clairvoyance involved diagnosing and curing patients with the assistance of spirits or by using an object close to the patient. A furious article in *The Age* in January 1872 complained that even physicians from the University of Melbourne were consulting a well-known medium. 'Seriously, we ask what is the profession coming to in this colony? Where is this demoralizing humbug to end?'

In the early 1890s, the land speculation bubble burst with drastic consequences: bank runs, financial collapses, panic, bankruptcies, unemployment. The prosperity of the 1880s had meant that more Melburnians could afford medical care, and the number of 'medical men' more than doubled over a decade, going from 202 to 420. After the crash, the number declined again. Perhaps some of the quacks were driven out, or sought more profitable pastures.

It's impossible to know for sure, but by 1891 Dr King and his institute had disappeared from the Russell Street address, which was now occupied (according to Sands & McDougall) by a Miss Frewen and a registry office, and no Dr Kings appeared in the list of medical practitioners. All that remained of Dr King was his advertising sign.

*

– *What happened to her after that, I wonder ...*

Agnes stands on the corner of Russell Street and Flinders Lane. Her youngest baby is in her arms, her three-year-old fretfully pulling at her hand. She is hot, exhausted and desperate: it has cost her the last of her savings to get here by train – her first ever trip on the new railway – in the hope of getting more of Dr King's elixir, or at least her money back. But now that she is here, the Australian Medical Institute – whose crest looked so impressive on the letter

– turns out to be a chimera. The brisk young lady at number 42 has never heard of the Institute or Dr King – she only took the lease a few weeks ago – looks askance at Agnes's unfashionable clothes, and notes her attitude of manic desperation. She seems to suspect Agnes of some immoral purpose, and asks her to leave. Agnes walks slowly along Russell Street, not knowing or caring where she is, only that her head is splitting, she has a craving she can never fulfil, and all her savings are gone.

Maybe she heads up Russell Street, over the hill, towards the opium dens of Little Bourke Street. Maybe she turns the other way and heads towards the Yarra. Or maybe she simply takes the train home to Kerang.

– *We will never know.*

*

Was that the last that Melbourne saw of Doctor King?

Although his name disappeared from the next few editions of the famous directory, a Dr King surfaced in 1895, this time associated with the 'Eclectic Remedy Agency' at 323 Collins Street.

'Eclectic medicine' was a popular therapy in the late nineteenth century. Originating in the United States, it was based on herbal remedies and was regarded by many as a legitimate school of medicine. To Melbourne's medical establishment, though, it would have been another variant of quackery. Was this the same man, making a brief attempt at a revival? Or was he a rival Dr King? Either way, the Eclectic Remedy Agency was short-lived. By 1897, it too had vanished, and no more Dr Kings appear in the Sands & McDougall directories during the late Victorian era.

I don't know whether there were two Dr Kings or just one. But I like to imagine them as the same person. The Dr King of my imagination is 'celebrated' more for his fast talking, brash persona and flashy, boom-town style than for his medical skills. These days he would have his own infotainment show in the small hours of the morning, specialising in erectile dysfunction, male baldness and miracle weight-loss treatments. Characters like him helped to define Melbourne in the 1890s, as the white-shoe brigade of corporate crooks defined the 1980s. Respectable city worthies are memorialised in statues and oil paintings, but the shameless Dr King popped up again in Russell Street to promote himself to Melburnians more than a century later.

What of the ghost sign? We went back a few months later to have another look. The new building – a Hellenic Cultural Centre – was well under way, and one of the site workers told us that Dr King's sign would be obliterated. 'That wall's coming down', he said. 'It's not structurally safe. Even if we saved it, no one would ever see it.' Shortly afterwards, the sign was gone.

That may be appropriate. Dr King wasn't exactly a long-standing pillar of the Melbourne community, but a dubious self-promoter who blazed across the city for a short time. So it's only fitting that his advertisement should share the same fate: reappear out of nowhere, trumpet his name down Russell Street for a few months, then disappear. This time for ever.

*

There is another footnote to this story. After my original article about Dr King was published, I was contacted by Gail Jones, novelist and scholar of psychogeography.

> I showed my mother – Noreen Jones (née King) – your article about the 'medical clairvoyant' doctor JW King; he is my mother's great great grandfather (my great,

> great great!) and she's done quite a bit of research on him and his son. If you need any more details her email is ... and she's happy to answer enquiries.
>
> I note you didn't find evidence of the doctor's training in London: that's because he trained in Dublin – the King family originated in Ireland.

This was too good an opportunity to pass up, so I contacted Noreen Jones who kindly provided me with the details of Dr King's life.

Born in 1822, James William King qualified as a surgeon in Dublin in 1849. (So my initial assumption was wrong, he wasn't exactly a quack – he was at least as well qualified as most doctors of the time.) By 1851, he was in Brixton, London, where his first son James Waterhouse King was born. The family then emigrated to Victoria, and by 1854, Dr King was living in Lennox Street, Richmond. A couple of years later, in 1856, he had settled in Kerang as a medical practitioner. Kerang, a very new settlement, had only existed for about a decade. Dr King seems to have been an energetic and entrepreneurial fellow (as his later advertising suggested) – just the man for a medical practice in the wild gold mining town of Bendigo, where he also had property and mining interests. During the 1860s and 1870s, he was active in and around Ballarat, served as a Justice of the Peace, and dipped his toe into politics as a nominee for Parliament. In his later years, he attempted to crack the Melbourne market, judging by the advertisement on Russell Street and the advertisement in the Emerald Hill newspaper, but basically his was a country practice. An obituary appeared in the *Bendigo Advertiser* on 23 May 1895, filed from Inglewood, a gold rush town north-west of Bendigo.

> Inglewood, Wednesday.
>
> DEATH OF A PIONEER. I notice that the death of

> Dr J.W. King, late of Ballarat, is announced in the metropolitan journals. The deceased resided and practised here for some time in the early days, but long before those times he was practising at Kerang South. From Kerang, the doctor came to Newbridge, where he practised until the discovery of Inglewood, to which place he came to follow his profession, and subsequently went to Ballarat, where he died as announced. The doctor when at Kerang was the only J.P. for miles around, and I learn was also a protector of the Aborigines for a very large district. He was an ardent sportsman and angler, and not long since he sent fish from Ballarat to stock our reservoir.

Noreen Jones pointed me towards a large advertisement in the *Bendigo Advertiser* in 1893 for the 'Electric Medical Institute' on Mitchell Street. Was this related to the 'Eclectic Remedy Agency' run by Dr King in Collins Street? The mystery was further compounded: was our friend electric or eclectic? Did a typo creep into Sands & McDougall? Or was Dr King simply diversifying?

The confusion is appropriate because he was a protean figure, frequently reinventing himself and his business. A new place lets you do that. No one knows you or cares about your history: you can become whoever you like. Call yourself a 'celebrated specialist', write it in letters ten feet high, and it becomes the truth. Melbourne in the nineteenth century, like any boom town, was full of Dr Kings: oddballs, chancers, con men and risk-takers. *O brave new world, that has such people in it!* How different to the 'Old World', where everyone knows you and your family, and your options are bounded in a nutshell. Dr King's ghost sign is more than an ad: it's emblematic of a culture.

SICILY ON LYGON STREET

We chance on the Stone Mill one afternoon as we wander down Lygon Street in Brunswick, and decide to stop for lunch. It's an Italian place, traditional, as we can tell by the old photographs lining its walls: family groups, workers, eager young faces looking fearlessly out from the black-and-white past. Seeing our interest, the Sicilian owner regales us with tales of who and what and where and when. I forget the details now. It's our own memories that matter.

Because it was in Italy we first got together. We met in England in 1988, both working as teachers at a summer school for European teenagers. After that, you had a teaching job organised in Cairo, while I had taken a position in Salerno near Naples. For several months we exchanged letters, getting to know each other through the pages of that thin blue air mail paper. One day I plucked up enough courage to invite you to visit me in Salerno. (There were a couple of weeks of suspense between my sending the invitation and your response landing in the little metal mailbox of the flats on via Moscati. How quaint that sounds now, in the age of instant clicks, like a relic from Jane Austen's day.) Anyway, you said yes.

I was supposed to meet you at Naples station, but there was some kind of mix-up and we missed each other. But you were a veteran traveller, and found your own way to the flat while I was out searching for you. We had a week together, taking drives along the Amalfi coast, where every corner brings a startling view of vertiginous drops and dazzling blue ocean. We walked together around the ruins of Pompeii, and kissed at the Greco-Roman ruins of Paestum. A photographic record exists of that moment, taken by a passing Italian guy, a romantic at heart, who directed us to kiss: *'Bacio! Bacio!'* he said, gesturing with his hands. We went to a restaurant for dinner, which was closed for a private function, but the family invited us in anyway, and small children played around our feet as we ate. After midnight we stood for a long time beside a little lake on the *lungomare* where ducks more suited to the rain were making the most of it. I was wet, worn out and puzzled. You were silent, thinking – you told me later – about whether you were ready to commit to a relationship. We made love for the first time in that little room in the back streets of Salerno. Early the next morning, I had to head off to my teaching job at the engineering company, but when I came home, you were standing on the balcony laughing and waving a handkerchief, playing up to the role of *signora*.

A curious thing happened one night at a bar in the old part of town, the *centro storico*. It was a medieval cellar, five or six centuries old, converted to a venue in which, that night in 1989, a band of local lads was playing covers of The Beatles, The Doors and Pink Floyd. At some point we noticed that the walls were adorned with a few posters – there was one of the pyramids of Egypt – and then you exclaimed 'My god, that's the tram I used to catch to Melbourne Uni.' I didn't even know that Melbourne had trams, but there it was, a poster of a tram – your tram – on the wall of a subterranean Italian bar. The three places – Salerno, Egypt, Melbourne – combined in a moment of synchronicity, drawing together past, present and future. In the months to come, I visited you in Cairo, and we saw the pyramids together, and later, when we came to Melbourne, we often rode that tram. At the time, it seemed a cosmic sign that we were meant to be together: at least, that's how we interpreted it. We remembered all this as we sat in the restaurant on Lygon Street.

– *How did we miss each other at the station?*

– *I don't know, but I was glad you went looking for me.*

– *I was worried.*

– *It's all right ... nothing ever happens to me.*

When your stint in Cairo finished, you moved to Italy, and we lived in Milan for almost a year, but that's another story. On that day in the Stone Mill, we were full of plans for our future. 'Sicily!' you said, looking up at the map on the wall. 'How come we've never been there?' We had read *Midnight In Sicily*, watched *Montalbano*. Sicily was ideal for people like us, obsessed by layers of time: its history involves centuries of successive invasions and occupations by Phoenicians, Greeks and Romans, Byzantines, Arabs, Normans, Spaniards and Italians. The map above us was a virtual invitation, but an actual invitation was issued soon enough by the restaurant owner, who gave us names and addresses of all his family (including first, second and third cousins), friends we could stay with, and associates who would drive us wherever we wanted to go. By the time the coffee arrived, we were sold. Why wait till we retired? We could go and live there in the next couple of years. You could pick up some teaching, I could write. It would be the perfect bookend to our relationship – or, better yet, a new chapter, a new start. In a new place, what people might we become? We spoke often over the next couple of years about Sicily, looked at each other over our coffee cups and mouthed the word, but the plan never progressed beyond that.

When couples know each other as well as we knew each other, and their memories are so knitted together, they don't need to make their thoughts explicit: each can tell by the other person's eyes what they are thinking. If we were watching television, and something came on about Pompeii, we didn't have to say anything: we'd glance at each other and our eyes would say 'Remember?' That's how it was, too, in that restaurant with the maps and photographs on the wall: a glance across the table brought back the ducks, the balcony, the bar, the kiss. In time, the Stone Mill itself and the conversation there became a memory. Now I am unpacking Russian dolls: memories within memories. I think myself forward to some future time when I will be in Sicily, and I will look back on myself writing this, remembering that conversation I had with you, when we had no idea what was to come.

And if I ever do go to Sicily, I'll be walking its streets with you. Together we'll visit the archaeological sites, the places where they filmed *Montalbano*, and perhaps find a restaurant with kids playing on the floor. And I'll turn to you and say 'Remember?'

WANDERING BRUNSWICK

Our original plan was to follow Robert MacFarlane's instructions to walk in a circle around the city. However, this becomes problematic when we think of the suburbs we would miss on the way. It seems foolish to walk through Carlton, Fitzroy and Collingwood, then continue east without a backward glance at suburbs like Brunswick, where there's so much to see. So we break our self-imposed rule, double back and make our way through a few slightly more northern suburbs. The shape of the final walk will end up more like a spider's web than a circle.

Leaving Parkville behind us, we cross Brunswick Road and tramp up Sydney Road into Brunswick. This familiar thoroughfare gives us the sense of being time-travellers as we walk through its mix of architecture: nineteenth century churches; a moderne apartment block that has seen better days (called 'Gladholme', it's not so glad today); the old mechanics' institute, built in 1868, now a performing arts centre; and the Brunswick Town Hall, an imposing Victorian edifice that was almost knocked down during the carnage of the 1970s. Brunswick is the burial ground of many Marvellous Melbourne buildings obliterated by Whelan the Wrecker. So significant a name in Melbourne was Whelan, that the firm has been the subject of a biography by Robyn Annear. Whelan's signage, ironically, remains.

The general vibe is cheap and cheerful, with a succession of nail salons, charity shops, discount places and fast food joints. There's a Savers, an Aldi and a Franco Cozzo, which takes care of clothes, food and furniture. The Hot Potatoes store, which once offered discount gifts and varieties, has now, as its signage disintegrates, become

OT PO AT S SCOUNT G TS V TIES.

Hipsterdom encroaches in the form of groovy coffee houses, vintage boutiques and bike shops. As we pass, the Uniting Church is offering a 'Blessing of the Bikes', in response to the recent death of a cyclist. Sydney Road is, indeed, a traffic nightmare and divine intervention seems almost a requirement to prevent fatalities.

Many of the Victorian shops along this strip carry the names of those who originally built and occupied them – Hennessys, Frazers, Ellemor – although those occupants have long since gone. Likewise, a few ghost signs linger on the walls, evoking names like Nestlé, Violet Crumble, Robur Tea. One of our favourites is the cute signage at number 159, which at first sight looks like 'Miss Reyon', but in fact is the name of a former occupant, Miss R. E. Yon. Today, Miss Yon has quite a fan following on the internet: she was in the fashion business in the 1920s, and a newspaper advertisement from 1923 reveals that she was a manufacturer and importer of stylish 'taffeta silk coats and crepe de Chine frocks', the kind of garments worn by Kerry Greenwood's glamorous detective Phryne Fisher. Nearby is a sign dating from the 1940s for Nissens lingerie, frocks, suits, hosiery, gloves, and coats.

A glance at Sands & McDougall suggests that Sydney Road hasn't changed that much over the years. Back in 1946, there were lots of dressmakers and hosiery makers on the street, along with cafés, grocers, hairdressers, jewellers and cycle shops. A little further up the street we reach the 'bridal belt'. Even on a Sunday afternoon, with the shops closed, groups of young women can be seen window-shopping at Glory Wedding, Belle et Blanc, Kylie Bridal, Lady Stardust, Duchess, and Made of Honour. It's not just frock shops: all the associated nuptial articles can be bought here, from cakes to stationery. There's even a costume jewellery shop with the intriguing name of Impostors. A shop for wedding crashers? Not in the market for bridal wear, we pop around the corner into Ballarat Street, and see a couple of interesting buildings on opposite sides of the street.

One is a modernist 1950s building, occupied by a succession of clothing manufacturers for more than 50 years. It was built during the post-war era, the time of ETA and Olex, when the manufacturing boom and architectural modernism briefly co-existed. You can make out a ghost sign for Perucci shirts on the wall, but before that it was occupied by other manufacturers. The building is in a sorry state now, but was once impressive – reminiscent of the peanut butter factory in Braybrook, though less acclaimed. The other building, a little further down Ballarat Street, is the former Brunswick Market, a Spanish Mission fantasia that couldn't be more different to the 1950s factory.

This is a well-known local landmark, although it only operated as a market for a couple of years. A retail entrepreneur opened the place in 1930, intending it to be a local alternative to Victoria Market. The Spanish Mission style, imported from California and Florida, was enjoying its Melbourne vogue at the time, and the striking design was meant to get people talking: it still stands out from all those square brick Victorian buildings surrounding it. But sustaining a new venture was challenging during the Depression and the market was gone by 1933. The building was subsequently used as a storage place and a box maker, but as we wander along Ballarat Street, we can still briefly imagine ourselves in California.

Further north, up the top end of Sydney Road, the vibe changes a little. There are more discount and bargain shops, and places with optimistic names like Liquidation House. There are kebab places and shisha lounges, and blokes chatting in Arabic outside cafés. We pass a shop with a window full of those flashing signs that say 'OPEN', but the shop itself has a photocopied sign on the door reading 'We are closed.' However, Maxine's Erotic Ultra Lounge is open, offering burlesque classes and buck's-night entertainment. There's a massive pink vinyl sign, from which Maxine, in a low-cut leopard-skin top nothing like Miss R E Yon's, beams down on the passing traffic.

From Sydney Road we head east along Blyth Street as far as Nicholson Street. Then we reach a place with more personal associations: Errol Avenue, where you lived in a share house as a student in the early 1980s. We hunt for a while, until you finally track it down. We stand outside and you tell me the story. You were one of those who benefited from Gough Whitlam opening up the tertiary education system in the 1970s: without that, you'd never have gone to university. You got out of the family home, just before your parents' marriage fell apart, to make your own way. You studied English and French, then a Dip Ed, while working part-time at Repat. The soundtrack was Split Enz, Mondo Rock and Vince Jones. The movies were *The Last Metro*, *Breaker Morant*, and *Gallipoli*. You read Hugo, Sartre, Maupassant, and even Mao (getting into an argument once on a tram because of it). You volunteered with the student counselling helpline, played tennis, and dressed up for *The Rocky Horror Show*. It was a student life like millions of others, but unique because it was yours. Many others have passed through Errol Avenue since then, but it will always be important in your story because it was your personal escape route. After you graduated, you sent a thank-you letter to Gough Whitlam. Amazingly, he replied by telegram: 'Letters such as yours make it all worthwhile congratulations'. You still have the telegram – a small yellow square addressed to you, including the post-nominal title BA. It's a form of communication that's now extinct, and Gough has gone too, but we have the telegram in a frame, a physical record of that era which you prize more than the degree itself.

There's a ghost sign at the corner of Overend and Church Streets that is a real test of the eyes. A Robur sign is visible, lower right. But what else? The wall was covered in signs at one point, but time and weather have done their job and nearly everything has been washed away. We stand for a long time, straining our eyes, trying to decode the tiny traces that remain. We reckon we can make out the name 'Bruce' and the words 'Cash grocer'. We can only imagine the brands that might have been visible here – Bushells tea, McAlpin's flour, perhaps Ecks lemonade or Velvet Soap? Now, almost nothing. Even the faint taste of Robur may be gone in a few more years. This is what happens when ghost signs are completely exposed to the elements, and even the wall loses its memory.

We imagine time lapse photography of the wall over the course of a century or so – bright new signs appear then fade, are replaced by a succession of new names, one on top of the other, as the shop changes hands and its occupants move on: blue names on red, white on black, like postage stamps on an envelope, until at a certain point the wall is left to itself and the signs melt away to nothing, leaving only amnesia. In a way, a blank wall is more evocative than one whose signs survive.

Not far away, in the side streets to the west of Lygon Street, are some more recent additions to the walls, in the form of galleries of street art. This type of expression was almost unknown in the 1930s, but the best of it is an enrichment to the city today. One could use these images as the starting point for many kinds of narrative: fairy tales, fantasy, erotica, surrealism, political satire. Among them we spot several by Baby Guerrilla, whose flying lovers we encountered in Footscray. Here she has created an airborne violinist, a line of flying children holding hands, a woman surrounded by birds. How long will these images survive? At a guess, longer than Maxine's Ultra Lounge ... perhaps not as long as Robur. You never know, though. If this street art is still here in fifty or a hundred years, what might future generations make of this painting by an unknown artist of Tony Abbott in his speedos astride a missile named 'Irony'? Perhaps some psychogeographer of the year 2116 will be as perplexed as we were by the suited monkey of Abbotsford Street.

Abbott and his speedos came back to haunt me later. After you died, I found an unsent email on your computer addressed to him. He had made an ignorant comment criticising the South Sudanese community, and you wanted to set him right.

> *Tony, I have worked with African migrants for many years ... The community includes a proud population of newly qualified lawyers, teachers, footballers, netball players and business people. When migrant kids came to English classes, many had disrupted schooling, so they needed a lot more time than they were funded for. Often they were abused in trains and on the streets. They have endured a lot of trauma, they endure more when politicians start generalising about them as a group.*

You had not quite finished the email, because by that stage you were losing your eyesight. But you never lost your sense of fairness, nor your habit of writing to former prime ministers. So that message was unsent. But I'm hitting Send now.

THREE GHOST SIGNS, THREE HISTORIES

The pace and nature of our walk varies from suburb to suburb. In some, we stride long straight roads, warehouses on either side of us, to a soundtrack of the airbrakes of trucks, and we walk quietly, each with our own thoughts. In others, we lose ourselves in quiet residential street after quiet residential street, where only by being alert to minute differences in sculpted bushes and garden ornaments can we tell one house from another. In Fitzroy, though, so many stories are tumbling off the walls that there's almost too much to see: the ghost signs are many and varied, the street art is rich and surreal. Angels perch above gratings, bright solar systems swirl across factories, zebras graze on cottages, and children's faces gaze solemnly from brick walls. What follows is just a sample of what we find.

C.W. PUGH, OPTICIAN

We spot him a few doors along Gertrude Street, at the entrance of a café at number 13. Unusually for ghost signs, it appears not on the wall but beneath our feet, telling us that this was once the premises of C.W. Pugh, optician. The marble mosaic is well preserved and quite beautiful with its simple sans serif lettering. That capital G in

Pugh's name looks odd – as if it was a C with a little tail added as an afterthought. A mosaic like this would surely be more expensive than a simple painted sign, so perhaps Mr Pugh was making a statement about the hoped-for prestige and permanence of his business.

What does Sands & McDougall have to say? C.W. Pugh, optician, moved into number 13 in 1898, and stayed there until 1908, after which another optician, Ernest MacFarlane, took over the shop – but didn't remove his predecessor's name, which has remained for more than a century after the man himself departed. Mr C.W. Pugh was a high-end optician, as his sign suggests. After all, he was at the fancy end of Gertrude Street, not far from the Exhibition Building. In 1898 and 1899, he placed advertisements in Sands & McDougall emphasising his elite clientele. Lord Brassey, his most celebrated client, was an English lord, and Governor of Victoria from 1895 to 1900. C.W. Pugh's occupancy was not particularly long: only ten years. His successor was much more enduring. As late as 1974 the shop at 13 Gertrude Street was still occupied by E.J. MacFarlane & Sons, opticians. But the mosaic remains, a memorial of sorts, though the feet of millions of passers-by have walked over it unheeding.

'OILY, BLACK AND BRILLIANT'

If C.W. Pugh was hobnobbing with the ruling classes, he was pretty unusual in Fitzroy, which has been a working-class suburb for most of its history. From Gertrude Street, we take a left, up Fitzroy Street, where we find an old boot polish factory. Eric Nicholls designed the factory in the 1920s – he was an architect in the office of Walter Burley Griffin, who with his wife Marion Mahony created a number of great buildings in Melbourne. Heritage listed, the building is a significant example of modernist design in the industrial sphere, like the ETA factory in Braybrook. A ghost sign appears on the front, the lettering formed out of detailed concrete:

JOSEPH LYDDY.: .O.B·B. POLISH MANUFR

Joseph Lyddy made polish for saddles and boots: the brand was associated with Cobb and Co coaches, provided polish to the Australian Light Horse Brigade during World War I, and apparently the name still exists today, although the company was taken over some years ago. But what does 'O.B.B' stand for? A search around

Trove yields the slogan, 'oily, black, and brilliant', which must have been so well known that it could be abbreviated. 'Give us a jar of the O.B.B., mate.'

INDEPENDENT HALL

A little further down Fitzroy Street, an odd little building proclaiming the name 'Independent Hall' catches our attention. It's now a private residence but the Gothic windows and doorway suggest a religious history. At the top right is an almost illegible ghost sign on which we can just make out the words 'Christian Endeavour' and something about times of services. Protruding from under the front wall's coping, there are three small busts of a steampunk-looking guy with a moustache. Who is he?

On the side wall is the vestige of another old sign: unfortunately tagged now, it offers a £5 reward for information about people 'scribbling' on the walls. At a best guess, the sign reads:

NOTICE
£5 REWARD

> Given to anyone with information about people damaging this property or trespassing on this property or scribbling on the walls

I don't know who you could claim the reward from these days, but in any case there has been a more spectacular addition to the wall: a mural of a surreal giraffe which extends its coiling neck and sinuous tongue across several metres.

The first mention of the Independent Hall (Fitzroy Mission) in Sands & McDougall was in 1908, at the same time as Mr Pugh was running his optician's business on Gertrude Street. If the ghost sign on the top right does indeed read 'Christian Endeavour', it's possible the hall was associated with the youth movement of that name that was active in Melbourne in the early twentieth century. However, by 1942 the hall was listed as vacant in Sands & McDougall. After World War II, it was converted to the Bethesda Aborigines Mission which operated from 1946–1954. It was run by Sister Maude Ellis, a deaconess in the Methodist church, who conducted church services, distributed food and clothing to the needy, and ran a kindergarten for about twenty children. By the mid-1950s the Bethesda Mission was no longer at the premises, and the hall was used for storage. Amazingly, the building survived the widespread 'clearances' that took place in Fitzroy in the 1950s and 60s, when much of the old suburb was swept away to make way for Housing Commission flats and car parks.

Finally, the place was sold and converted into a private residence. Since then, it has caught the eye of film and TV producers: keen-eyed readers of my blog pointed out that it has been used as a location in the Jack Irish drama series based on the novels of Peter Temple, starring Guy Pearce. Jack and his friends are fond of lamenting how the Fitzroy of old has been swept away by gentrification, but today you can still find countless traces pointing back to the suburb's past.

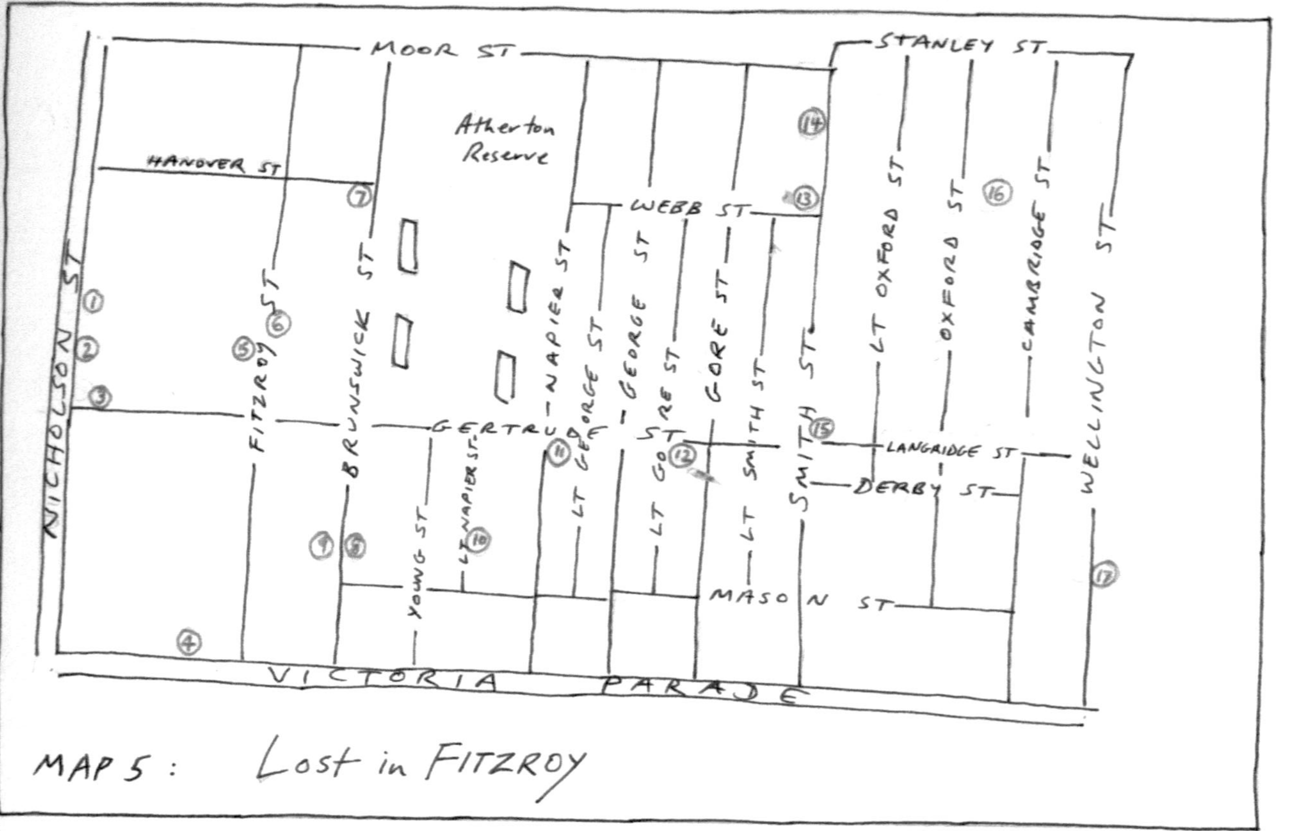

MAP 5: Lost in FITZROY

MAP 5.
LOST IN FITZROY

(1) The Cairo apartments, built in 1936, one of the earliest examples of apartment living in Melbourne.

(2) In contrast, Grantown House, spectacular ramshackle Victoriana.

(3) Mr Pugh's mosaic.

(4) Another Indian Root Pills ghost sign, high up on Victoria Parade.

(5) The Lyddy Polish building, with its mysterious OBB.

(6) Independent Hall.

(7) On Brunswick Street high up on the Hanover Street corner: a Rheem ghost sign.

(8) Ghost sign for the Hospital for Horses and Dogs.

(9) Once-grand architecture of Barcelona Terrace.

(10) More ghost signs on Little Napier Street.

(11) One of the best of Fitzroy's ghost signs is Vi-Lactogen on the east wall of an old pharmacy on Gertrude Street (Winfields is on the west wall.)

(12) The dead neon sign of Johnstone's store on Gertrude Street.

(13) Ghost sign of Patersons department store.

(14) Hannaford's pianos, with another mosaic, this time for Maples pianos.

(15) Ghost sign of Foresters Hall, another old friendly society.

(16) Between Oxford and Cambridge Streets, the buildings of the Foy & Gibson complex, with many ghost signs, now apartments.

(17) A well preserved ghost sign: 'Brewers and grains'.

ICONS OF CREMORNE

Cremorne is a tiny handkerchief of a suburb tucked into a pocket of land south of Richmond and north of the River Yarra and the Monash Freeway. This little area of narrow streets, red bricks and bluestone laneways was once a hub of industry, and the home of products that were literally household names: among them were Bryant and May matches and Rosella tomato sauce. (One might have used a Bryant and May match to light an Electrine candle: illumination made in Melbourne.) But the light went out a long time ago, and it's many years since those iconic products were actually made here.

In the 1850s, this suburb was home to the Cremorne Pleasure Gardens, the origin of the suburb's present name, set up by a theatrical entrepreneur who filled the place with tightrope walkers, trapeze artists, fireworks displays, dramatic panoramas of historical events, and the first balloon flight in Australia. These days, it is hip design studios, furniture makers, event managers, creative agencies, a place called 'Hotel de Cat' which seems to be a hotel for ... er ... cats, and cafés offering 'bespoke espresso'.

Cremorne has undergone a few transitions, but to wander around it today is to be confronted at every step by its industrial past. Perhaps the most celebrated icon of that past is the Nylex Plastics advertising sign and clock, perched atop the silos of a brewing company. It was erected in the 1960s, at a time when skysigns were a popular form of advertising. Many such skysigns have gone, but Nylex survives, and is listed on the Victorian Heritage Register. Over the past few years, there has been a bitter battle over the development of the silos, and how the sign should be preserved. Nylex Plastics is out of business, but the sign grows ever more famous, despite the fact that neither it nor the clock have functioned for years. The clock was famously mentioned in the song 'Leaps And Bounds' by another Melbourne icon, Paul Kelly, who performed on top of the silo in the song's video in the 1980s. So connected is the sign with the song (at least in our minds) that it's hard to think of one without the other. For us as for many Melburnians, Paul Kelly was part of the soundtrack of our lives around that time, when you couldn't go to a party or festival, turn on the radio or *Rage* without hearing his voice. Music, architecture and history come together on this spot.

Not far away, tucked down Dover Street, is another iconic neon sign: Slade Knitwear. Erected in 1970, it too has remained un-illuminated since the mid-1990s. Nevertheless, we stand there on Dover Street and crane our necks up at its impressive scale. A group of local activists fighting to preserve it took the name of RING (Residents in a Neon Glow). Accordingly, it was celebrated in Hayden Dewar's mural, painted on the side of yet another icon, the old Dimmeys store.

Turning from neon to paint, on Balmain Street we see the fading remains of the Rosella preserving company, which produced jams and tinned fruit, and until quite recently, tomato sauce for every Aussie barbecue – and what could be more iconic than that? According to Janet McCalman's history of Richmond, *Struggletown*, the Rosella preserving and canning factory was a major source of employment for young women. But the work was seasonal and insecure, and piece work favoured the young and strong who could work fast. Knowing that Richmond contained a large pool of people desperate for jobs, the company could always find casual labour when it needed it – especially in times of hardship.

When the company finally closed, there was much public lamenting at the loss of another 'Aussie icon'. (Also lots of 'outsauced' jokes.) You can still buy Rosella products, although of course the brand is now owned by an overseas company, like ETA peanut butter. Another major local employer was Bryant and May, the British match manufacturer, which produced Redhead matches. Its complex is a magnificent set of industrial red brick buildings, built in the early twentieth century, including a chimney monogrammed with the letters B & M, and a clock that, instead of numbers, has letters that spell out the name of the company. As with the Sands & McDougall building, there was an expectation of permanence about the business: its builders imagined it having no other future.

Bryant and May was a long established British company that had been the object of the 'matchgirls' strike' in London in the 1880s. Workers protested against the use of white phosphorus, which caused employees to develop appalling diseases, in particular a potentially fatal bone disease known as 'phossy jaw'. By the time the Melbourne factory opened, white phosphorus had been banned. The new product, using alternative chemicals, was called 'safety matches', as it was less dangerous to workers and less prone to explode in your pocket. Working conditions at Bryant and May's were regarded as generous by the standards of the time, and it was considered a 'model factory'. Janet McCalman writes: 'The large modern factories mollified their legions of semi-skilled and unskilled hands with good working conditions and plentiful organised recreation.' In the 1920s, that included picnics, competitive sports and Christmas parties. There are even tennis courts and, just off Church Street, a hall for social events called Brymay Hall.

Match production was extinguished in the 1980s, and Redheads today come from Sweden. A bored security guard, with whom you get into conversation, tells us that the buildings are now owned by ANZ, whose plans for them are unclear.

Another iconic image is found on the rear of a wall in Cubitt Street, though the best view is to be had from the train line. It shows a footy player in a big V jumper (indicating that he was playing for the Victorian representative side, a tradition that was benched a couple of decades ago), mid-kick, with impressively bulging thighs and small pointed toes like a ballet dancer.

Like many places in Richmond and elsewhere, what looks like a former factory has been converted into a residence, but the current occupants have retained the sign, rather than thoughtlessly painting over it, as often happens. We spend ages peering through a wire fence at the back of a car park, looking across towards Cubitt Street and trying to decipher the words around the figure. Concentrating hard, we can see the almost vanished letters V. CAPONIO beneath the player's grounded boot. But Google uncovers no Victorian player called V. Caponio. Who is this elusive guy?

I post a story about the sign on my blog, but it seems that the footballer's identity will remain a mystery, until the Richmond and Burnley Historical Society puts me in touch with the family of the former factory's owner. I learn that Vincenzo Caponio, an Italian migrant, established and ran the family business, Champion Sporting Goods, which made soles and studs for football boots. So the name 'V. Caponio' on the sign is that of the founder of the company, not the footballer.

Vincenzo arrived in Australia in 1949 in response to an advertisement for toolmakers. He noticed that there was a gap in the market for quality studs in football boots, and with his wife Rina began to assemble them individually from scraps of leather and nails compressed on a swing press. The machines got bigger, the process evolved and the company grew until it was a major supplier to boot manufacturers. Champion moved into the Richmond premises – an old warehouse – in the early 1970s, which is when the sign was painted. Vince Caponio was an important employer and supporter of the Italian migrant community. The business thrived for a while but was hit hard in the 1980s, when tariffs were lifted and footwear manufacturing was largely booted offshore (a similar fate befell Bradmill, the clothing factory near our house).

Vince's son, Fabrizio, tells me that the sign was an artist's impression of Alan Martello, who played for Hawthorn in the 1970s, then switched to Richmond for three seasons. Martello was known as 'a prodigious kicker of the football' and he certainly looks it in photographs of the time – wearing boots with Champion studs. When Martello's image was transposed onto the Cubitt Street wall, from where he booted the footy far over the train line, something happened to him: his thighs bulged out like chicken drumsticks and his boots – originally the focus of the picture – shrank away to almost nothing. But that's part of the charm of the painting. The player frozen mid-kick is certainly unrecognisable as Martello. Nevertheless, his career continues after almost fifty years: a relic of a time when manufacturing, advertising and football were significantly different to what they are today. It may not be as celebrated as the Skipping Girl or Nylex signs, but the Wall of Champions seems just as iconic to us.

Some cities' icons celebrate centuries of history, spectacular architecture or natural beauties, great events or military victories. Melbourne's are more low-key. We don't make a big deal of an opera house or harbour, or put an admiral on top of a column. Neon signs and a clock, a bottle of sauce, and boxes of matches are among our most revered symbols. Sure, they're often commercial logos, but they represent simple pleasures, daily work and ordinary suburban life (the Nylex sign, hardly a thing of beauty in itself, is only celebrated because so many people drive past it on their way to and from work). Paul Kelly, whose songs are about the ordinary heartbreaks of life, seems typically Melburnian in a way that a more flamboyant performer never would.

These icons remind us of the people who built businesses and lives and communities, worked hard during the week, and ate pies and sauce at the footy on weekends. That's the basis of their emotional pull. In contrast, it's hard to feel anything about a product that is just another part of the global economy. We will never sigh over the loss of Google or Uber, ASOS or McDonalds. Perhaps what we forlornly try to hang on to – in our nostalgic attachment to these icons – is a time when everything wasn't so disconnected.

Finally, still in Cremorne, we come across a spectacular artwork by street artist Adnate, whose depictions of Indigenous children are a reminder of the land's original ownership and the fact that all these icons, however treasured, are but recent arrivals.

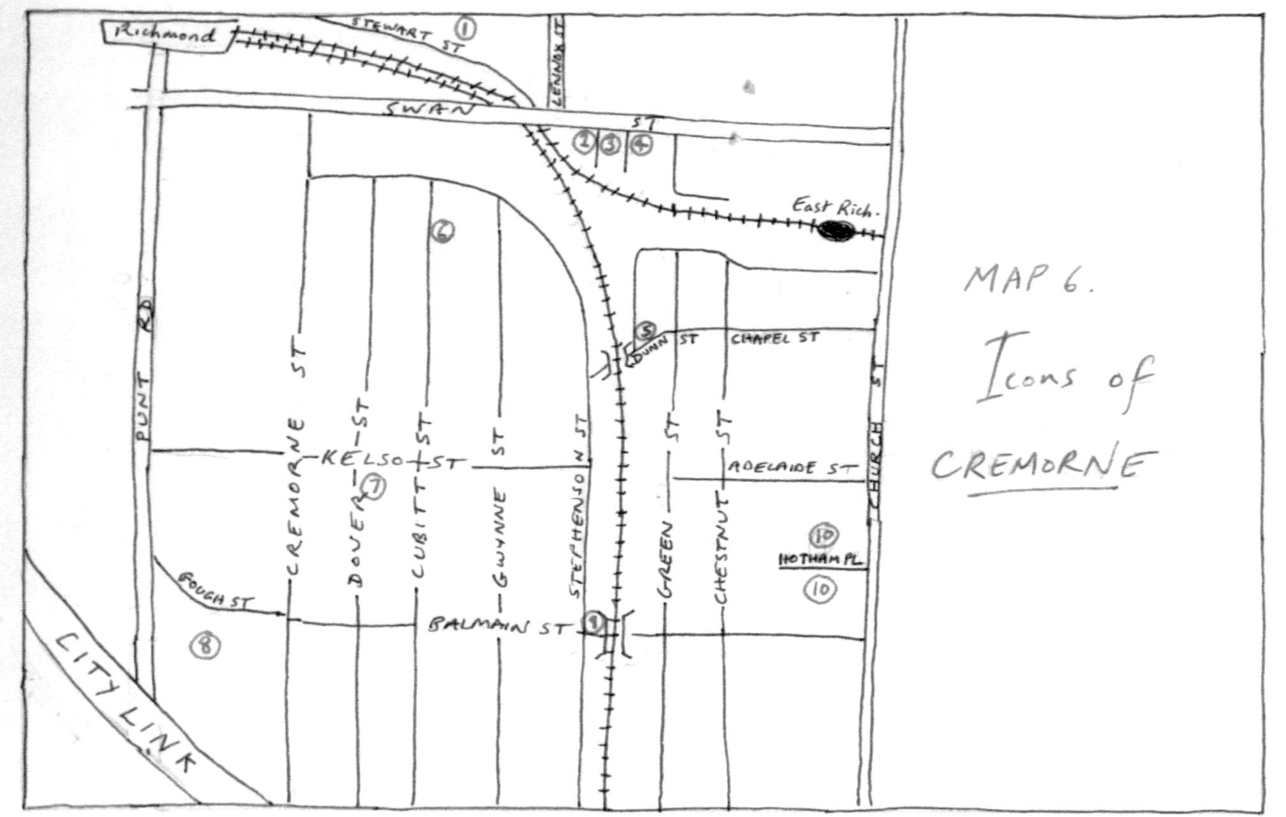
MAP 6.
Icons of CREMORNE
Richmond
East Rich.
STEWART ST
LENNOX ST
SWAN ST
PUNT RD
CITY LINK
CHURCH ST
CREMORNE ST
DOVER ST
CUBITT ST
GWYNNE ST
STEPHENSON ST
GREEN ST
CHESTNUT ST
KELSO ST
BALMAIN ST
GOUGH ST
ADELAIDE ST
CHAPEL ST
DUNN ST
HOTHAM PL

MAP 6.
ICONS OF RICHMOND AND CREMORNE

(1) Close to Richmond Station, the old Australian Knitting Mills have been converted to apartments: ghost signs for famous brands, Golden Fleece and Kookaburra, are visible, along with an impressive vertical arrow pointing to 'A.K.M.'.

(2) On Swan Street, ghost signs of the Maples Piano store, once known across Melbourne, are still prominent.

(3) The Monte de Piete at 138 Swan Street was one of a chain of pawn shops (there is another in Footscray): its signage can be seen from Byron Street. There is a gallery of layered ghost signs on the back wall: Penfolds wine and others relating to the Monte de Piete and the bottle shop next door.

(4) The former Dimmeys building with its landmark clock tower; along the side wall, a mural by Hayden Dewar is packed with local and national identities.

(5) Crossing the railway line at Green Street, a ghost sign reading 'Hairdresser' is visible on Dunn St.

(6) At the rear of 21 Cubitt Street, a ghost sign of the Champion footballer used to be visible.

(7) The Slade Knitwear skysign.

(8) The Nylex clock on top of the silos (marked Barrett Burston).

(9) The surviving facade of the Rosella factory with fading signage of eponymous rosellas.

(10) The substantial Bryant and May complex, including its clock tower with letters instead of numbers.

Street art in Cremorne, by Adnate

HOLLYWOOD ON THE YARRA

The urban landscape changes dramatically when we cross the river at Hoddle Bridge and move from Richmond into South Yarra. It almost feels like we are walking into a different city, in a different time. The contrast could hardly be starker: behind us are red-brick factories and giant silos, and the rows of houses once occupied by workers at Rosella and Bryant and May, while ahead of us are spectacular buildings in an array of architectural styles: streamlined moderne, deco, Spanish Mission, Californian, and more. Stratton Heights looks like an ocean liner about to steam off into the Yarra River, while others seem to be set in some unclear but romantic place and time. Most of these are the work of an entrepreneurial architect named Howard Lawson, Melbourne's most active flat developer of this period, who styled himself 'the architect who builds'.

Melbourne was built on waves of prosperity and recession. In common with much of the world, one of its bleakest periods was the Depression of the 1930s, which brought widespread unemployment and poverty. If you were a worker in the western suburbs, maybe you tried raising and racing greyhounds at White City to put food on the table. But life wasn't equally hard for everyone. If you were a bright young thing, with money and a liking for the glamorous life, there were numerous ways to indulge your fancies. You could go to one of Melbourne's new deco cinemas, like The Sun in Yarraville and The Astor in Prahran. And you might participate in the new trend – apartment living – that was taking off in Melbourne and Sydney. For many years, the ambition of most Australians had been to live in their own home on a quarter-acre block. In the 1930s, apartment living became a trendy option and fashionable young people embraced it – especially in well-heeled suburbs like South Yarra and Toorak. Art critic Basil Burdett wrote at the time, 'Melbourne has taken to flats with some of the feverish eagerness of a teetotaller converted to liquor'.

Traditional architects regarded Lawson's designs as bizarre parodies of architectural styles. Modernists, inspired by the Bauhaus with its clear geometric lines and lack of ornamentation, were equally contemptuous. The young Robin Boyd – a colleague of Frederick Romberg, who designed the ETA factory – voiced his contempt of suburban taste in his book *The Australian Ugliness*, proclaiming that the 'inglorious reign of the luxury flat ... [is] as bad from a social viewpoint as it is ridiculous from an aesthetic viewpoint.' You can't imagine anything more different from the ETA factory, or Romberg's Stanhill flats, than the fantastic Moorishness of Dorrington House, with its decorated cement facade, barley sugar columns, evocative archways and romantic staircases. No wonder modernists hated it – this is exactly the kind of mad eclecticism that Robin Boyd railed against. All the same, it's worth a long look.

Like many of Lawson's buildings, it was built on a slope, and makes ingenious use of staircases, pillars and balconies.

One might expect that building apartments in South Yarra was a path to a fortune, but Lawson spent most of the 1930s bankrupt, due to unwise investments in theatres and dance halls. Although he didn't create a business empire, his name lives on in Lawson Grove, which contains more of his buildings. Wandering up this quiet cul de sac, we imagine for a few moments that we might be in some corner of the Mediterranean, like one of those villas on the Amalfi coast we visited many years ago. The combination of balconies and staircases, the patterned circle on the balustrades (one of Lawson's calling cards), even the faux-Gothic lettering used for the building's names give them a kind of fictional quality, like places we might see in a film, or in someone's old home movie. It's easy to visualise ghosts or time travellers materialising on those balconies, flitting up the steps or through the archways. We imagine them haunted by shadowy Bright Young Things, the *entre-deux-guerres* generation indulging themselves with cars and cocktails as the world cruised towards disaster.

Perhaps the most extravagant of Lawson's creations is Beverley Hills on Darling Street, which consists of two large apartment blocks. The name is obviously meant to evoke the glamour of Hollywood, and perhaps the people who lived here did think of themselves as film stars as they sipped martinis on their balconies or wallowed in 'Ye Olde Swimming Pool'. These days, there's a romantic faded glamour about the place. We ascend long flights of steps between Spanish-style columns and ornamented balconies bedecked with vegetation, until we reach the tiny, circular swimming pool. It's hardly big enough to swim in, but you could certainly lounge there with a Manhattan.

Wandering up Lawson Grove, we stumble on a secret, tiny café, hidden in a dark recess on the ground floor of one of his buildings. It feels like another personal discovery, though many others have made it before us. We order coffee and talk with excitement about this oddball architect who brought the exotic styles of the world to Melbourne in the 30s.

> – *It would have been great for young women ... a chance to live independently.*

Your words evoke the thousands of young secretaries and nurses and teachers and business women who might have had their first taste of independence in flats like these. Then you tell me about when you moved away from Melbourne for the first time, to take up your teaching job in Wodonga. You were nervous as you made the long drive north-east in your old Holden, but excited by the prospect of a new life. At home your dad was in control, *always* in control, but you'd said goodbye to your family, to Repat, to study: for the first time you were doing what you really wanted. You found a room in a house owned by a guy who seemed respectable and professional, but on moving in, you discovered he was a pothead with cupboards full of plants. You had no particular moral objection, but it wasn't a good look for a first-year teacher to rock up to class reeking of dope, so you quickly moved out and found your own place. *My very own FLAT!* After paying the bond, you were down to your last 40 cents, but you'd never felt such elation. Your own place, your own career, your own life: that's what a flat represented to you. And perhaps some of the occupants of these flats in Lawson Grove felt that way too.

Lawson may have been a maverick and a bankrupt. But if an artist is someone who has a vision and follows it through despite opposition, then he deserves the name. There's a romantic madness about these buildings that sets them apart from anything else in Melbourne. In his eclectic pillaging from different styles, he came up with something perversely original. Not everyone could afford to live in them, of course. Many Melburnians of the time had to make do with sub-standard accommodation. But as an experiment in higher density living they were a fascinating addition to the city. And compared with the kind of nondescript shoddy apartments that are being built by the thousands these days, we'd rather live in one of these.

When I post an article about these buildings on my blog it attracts dozens of comments from people who remember living in the flats, or still do, and speak nostalgically of its community of artists, dancers, and actors, and the parties. 'The pool with its roman bridge was hugely popular and very well used in summer, and was always lit at night – I loved looking down on it from my bedroom balcony.' How enticing that sounds; how remote from the tedium of workaday life. Glamour on a small scale, perhaps; it was hardly Hollywood, but it was here, in the midst of the suburbs: a hint of romance, a taste of freedom.

LOST LETTERS

Not far from Lawson's extravagant fantasies, another architectural surprise awaits us. Heading east along Toorak Road, with its mainly Victorian shop fronts, we reach the former South Yarra Post Office, where we pause. Post offices these days are functional places, with little sense of a special mission, and often no different to any other shop ... but this? Its external walls are a gallery of carvings, decorative motifs of marsupials, emus, lizards, snakes, cockatoos, gumnuts and other Australian flora. The carvings are subtle, delicate: obviously the work of skilled craftsmen. But this place was built in the midst of the great crash of the 1890s when banks closed their doors, unemployment rose, and the population of the city dropped by about fifty thousand. Even so, in the midst of the crisis, they still managed to build this. Maybe such iconography on a public building fostered a sense of national identity in the years leading up to federation. And what it still says to us is: post offices *matter*. How many love letters, proposals, tragedies, announcements, declarations, letters from home and overseas, telegrams and headlines passed through this building? It was a clearing house for stories great and small.

– *Letters played a part in our story too.*

Shortly after we first met, in 1988, you went to Cairo, where you had already accepted a teaching position, and I went to the south of Italy, where I had taken a job. That was when, on separate continents, we began writing letters to each other on wafer-thin light-blue airmail paper. You told me about your life in Cairo: the crazy excessive expat scene that you viewed with a sceptical eye, the students that you loved, the teeming city outside your window, the feluccas on the Nile, the morning calls to prayer, the caretaker in a djellabah who slept outside your building, the words of Arabic you were starting to learn, your visits to the pyramids, Coptic monasteries and the temple of Rameses at Aswan. Later, I would see it for myself, but your penned words brought it to life for me, and more importantly brought *you* to life – your optimism and humour, and your endless fascination with the world. In one of my letters to you, I wrote the fateful words 'I'd like to see you again, perhaps we could fix it for the spring?' And you replied ...

I wish I could quote from your letters at this point, but I no longer have them. We did see each other in the spring, and much followed from that, but we moved between Italy and England a few times, for work and pleasure, before we came to Australia, and somewhere along the way your letters – bundled up together – were mislaid. I can hardly believe that I was so careless with something so precious. But spectacular carelessness was a mark of my youthful self: when we were on a flight between Melbourne and Malaysia, en route to England to get married, I managed to lose my flight tickets *on the flight itself,* necessitating an interview with a stony-faced official in dark glasses and uniform at Kuala Lumpur airport, flanked by men with guns. He let us proceed only after you tearfully explained that we would miss our wedding otherwise. One of the gunmen whispered to us: 'My boss is feeling very soft because you mentioned a wedding', but not a muscle flickered in the hatchet-like face. So it's not altogether surprising that I managed to lose your letters, although I would give anything to have them back now. As we spent the next thirty years together, and people who are together do not write letters to each other, or even postcards, I have practically nothing that you wrote to me. You, of course, kept the letters I wrote to you: here they are, in your bedside drawer. But I don't want to read those, I am sick of the sound of my own voice.

What I want is to hear yours again, but it's lost, along with the letters.

*

Other things have been lost during the history of Melbourne's postal system. These days, on the rare occasions that we still receive letters and postcards, they arrive addressed with our suburb and its four-digit postcode: Yarraville 3013. We have had a few others in our time: Blackburn South 3130, Burwood 3125, East St Kilda

3183. But those numbers are not what we see if we turn back the clock and peer into an old newspaper or Sands & McDougall. For much of the twentieth century, Melbourne's suburbs had a postcode modelled on the London system. From 1928 to 1967, Footscray was W11, Hawthorn E2, and St Kilda S2.

The now-abandoned system of postal districts worked on a simple and intuitive code: N = north, S = south, SE = south-east, W = west, E = east, C = central, SC = south central. Each of the main districts was subdivided by number. Roughly speaking, the higher the number, the further out you were from the city centre. An article in *The Argus* of 11 January 1928 explained the rationale for adopting such a system: 'for the purpose of facilitating and reducing the cost of handling mails' the metropolitan area was divided into 104 areas 'based on that used in London'. Once the new codes were in use, there would be no need to add the name of the suburb. The scheme was needed, it was explained, because 'at present many letters are addressed to the wrong suburbs', such as Elwood instead of St Kilda. It is unclear why this happened, or why it was thought people would be more likely to write a postcode correctly rather than a suburb name, but there you go.

The system survived pretty much unchanged for almost forty years, until it was abolished and replaced by Australia-wide postcodes in 1967, shortly after the conversion from British pounds sterling to decimal currency. It's tempting to see the repudiation of both systems as symbolic of a belated desire for national independence. All the same, I think the old approach had something to commend it. If someone tells us they live in Kingsville, Hughesdale, or Merlynston, how do we know where that is? Adding the current postcode, Kingsville 3012, is not much help. If they said 'Kingsville W12' 'Hughesdale SE12' or 'Merlynston N14' then we would immediately have a rough idea of where they were residing.

But if we'd kept the old postal districts, imagine how much

snobbery would be attached to them; how much the already inflated price of real estate would be exaggerated by the addition of an 'SE'! As in London, people would kill for a flat in the fashionable district. Social climbers would refuse to date anyone with an N or W postcode. But the Ws and Ns would fight back: young writers from the west would defiantly start a lit mag called 'W13'; artists from the northern suburbs would show in a gallery space called 'N19' ...

The old post offices, like the old post codes, are mostly gone now; though some, like the South Yarra Post Office, survive as heritage spaces. Another is the former post office on Little Bourke Street. These days, there's a retail mega hub in the old GPO building, full of cafés and designer clothes – and nothing as quaint as mail sorting goes on there. But casting our eyes up above the international brand names at ground level, we catch sight of a faded ghost sign with the words 'letter delivery'. We imagine, for a moment, long-gone postmen plodding around N12 and SE5, C1 and W13. Like the Sands & McDougall team, they were professional walkers. Did they know the district codes by heart, murmuring them like a mantra as they walked their rounds? Do the codes live on in the memories of elderly residents, becoming fainter and fainter with the passing of years? When was the last time W11 appeared on an envelope? Like the lost names of Melbourne, the ghostly postcodes linger faintly on the map, known only, if at all, to a dwindling few.

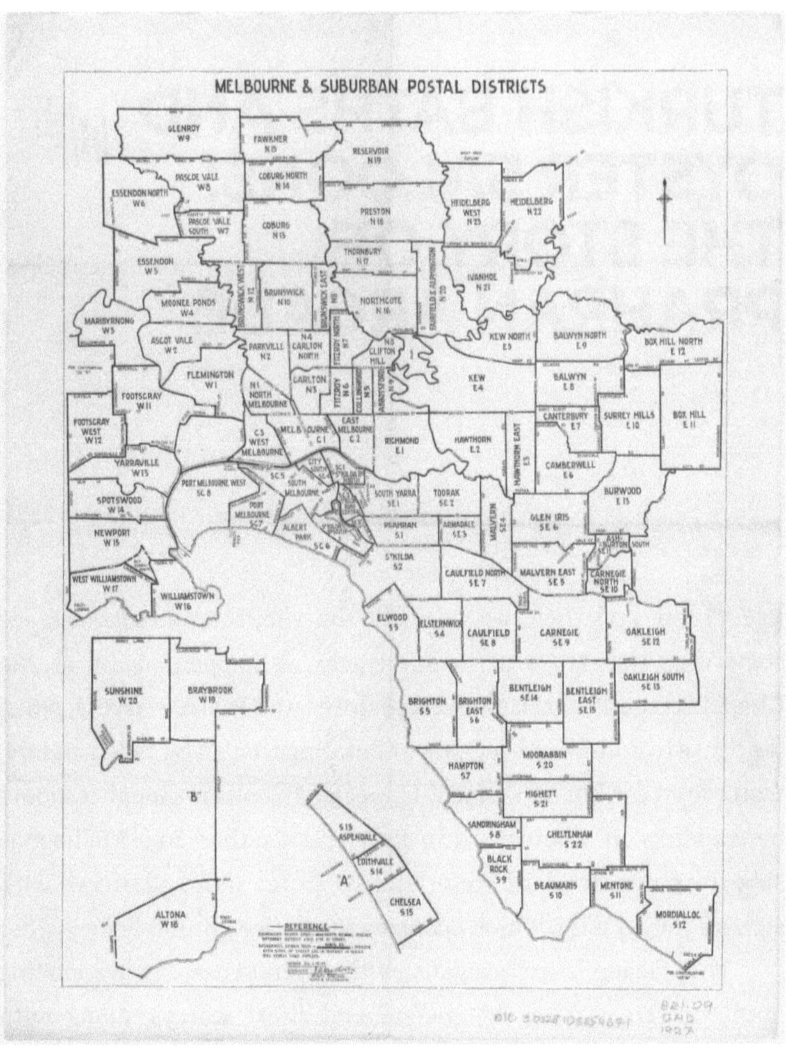
MELBOURNE & SUBURBAN POSTAL DISTRICTS
GLENROY W9
FAWKNER N15
RESERVOIR N19
PASCOE VALE W8
COBURG NORTH N14
ESSENDON NORTH W6
PASCOE VALE SOUTH W7
COBURG N13
PRESTON N18
HEIDELBERG WEST N23
HEIDELBERG N22
ESSENDON W5
THORNBURY N17
BRUNSWICK WEST N12
BRUNSWICK N10
BRUNSWICK EAST N11
NORTHCOTE N16
FAIRFIELD & ALPHINGTON N20
IVANHOE N21
MOONEE PONDS W4
MARIBYRNONG W3
ASCOT VALE W2
PARKVILLE N2
N4 CARLTON NORTH
FITZROY NORTH N7
N8 CLIFTON HILL
KEW NORTH E5
BALWYN NORTH E9
BOX HILL NORTH E12
FLEMINGTON W1
N1 NORTH MELBOURNE
CARLTON N3
FITZROY N6
COLLINGWOOD N5
ABBOTSFORD N9
KEW E4
BALWYN E8
FOOTSCRAY W11
FOOTSCRAY WEST W12
C3 WEST MELBOURNE
MELBOURNE C1
EAST MELBOURNE C2
RICHMOND E1
HAWTHORN E2
HAWTHORN EAST E3
CANTERBURY E7
SURREY HILLS E10
BOX HILL E11
CAMBERWELL E6
YARRAVILLE W13
PORT MELBOURNE WEST SC8
SC5
SOUTH MELBOURNE
SOUTH YARRA SE1
TOORAK SE2
MALVERN SE4
BURWOOD E13
SPOTSWOOD W14
PORT MELBOURNE SC7
ALBERT PARK SC6
PRAHRAN S1
ARMADALE SE3
GLEN IRIS SE6
NEWPORT W15
ST KILDA S2
ASHBURTON SE11
SOUTH
WEST WILLIAMSTOWN W17
WILLIAMSTOWN W16
CAULFIELD NORTH SE7
MALVERN EAST SE5
CARNEGIE NORTH SE10
ELWOOD S3
ELSTERNWICK S4
CAULFIELD SE8
CARNEGIE SE9
OAKLEIGH SE12
SUNSHINE W20
BRAYBROOK W19
OAKLEIGH SOUTH SE13
BENTLEIGH SE14
BENTLEIGH EAST SE15
BRIGHTON S5
BRIGHTON EAST S6
MOORABBIN S20
HAMPTON S7
"B"
HIGHETT S21
S13 ASPENDALE
SANDRINGHAM S8
CHELTENHAM S22
EDITHVALE S14
BLACK ROCK S9
"A"
BEAUMARIS S10
MENTONE S11
CHELSEA S15
ALTONA W18
MORDIALLOC S12
REFERENCE

TURKISH BATHS AND OYSTER SALOONS: THE STORY OF PRAHRAN ARCADE

Every now and then, as we walk the suburban streets, we see something that stops us in our tracks. It happens again at 282 Chapel Street, Prahran, between Princes and Walker Streets, when we pause to admire a three-storey building that's a bit faded and the worse for wear, but unmistakably special. It looks as though it should be standing on a boulevard in Paris, rather than in a Melbourne suburb among standard Victorian two-storey shops, plastered with signage for JB HiFi, which occupies the entire ground floor.

This facade is extravagant, with seventeen archways looking onto the street from the second and third storeys, along with columns and balconies, carved eagles, and a dizzying assortment of shells and other ornamentation. Clearly, it was once a place of note, but today it's a tatty anachronism – on first glance, anyway.

We go into JB HiFi and stickybeak around. Lifting our eyes above the displays of One Direction and *Breaking Bad*, we can see a high vaulted roof, more archways, and elegant cast ironwork. Clearly, this was no private house: it was a former shopping arcade. Like flaneurs – those dilettante wanderers of the nineteenth century – we stroll along the aisles, craning our necks upwards, trying to picture what used to be here. You spot him first – high up, on one of the inside windows – a faded, dusty man-in-the-moon smiles down at the shoppers, unnoticed by practically all. Is he a surviving relic of the building's Victorian origins, or a more recent addition?

On Chapel Street these days, New Age crystal vendors rub shoulders with boutiques, op shops, bars, second-hand bookshops, arts spaces and vintage dealers. But for many years it was a centre of mainstream retail that rivalled Bourke Street. Large department stores – The Big Store, Love and Lewis, and Read's furniture and drapery – still proudly proclaim their names to Chapel Street, although the retailers that bore those names have long gone. But before there were department stores, there were shopping arcades.

The early-to-mid nineteenth century was the golden age of arcades. These fantastic creations of glass, marble and wrought iron – stuffed full of luxury goods, such as silk and slippers, rubies and chocolates, corsets and carpets – were enchanted palaces to the shoppers of western cities. During this era, the fetish of the commodity rose to new heights. Walter Benjamin, the philosopher who made a study of arcades, wrote that they represented 'the enthronement of the commodity and the glitter of distraction around it'. Melbourne was not immune to this international craze, although as usual we got into it a bit late. Ever since the Great Exhibition of 1880 – for which the Royal Exhibition Building was built – middle-class Melburnians had displayed a voracious appetite for luxury goods, especially if imported. Today, only a handful of arcades survive in Victoria, the finest of which are the Block Arcade (built around the same time) and Royal Arcade, both in the CBD. Of the few built in the suburbs, the most significant was the Prahran Arcade.

The architectural style which had struck us on first glance (Those columns! The ornamentation! The statues! The eagles!) is known as Second Empire, popular in France during the time of Napoleon III (1852–70). Paris was the epitome of the sophisticated shopping city, the centre of luxury and fashion, and its arcades were a marvel: so it was fitting that Melbourne architect George McMullen chose this flamboyant style when he designed an arcade intended to rival those of Paris, London and New York. A photograph taken early in the building's life shows that it used to have a mansard roof with towers, which would have added to the visual impact. At some stage, though, it was scalped, and the name 'Prahran Arcade' was removed from below the pediment. There also used to be intriguing sculpted figures on either side of the front door, but if they are still there today, they are hidden behind JB's signage. A ghost sign on the side wall reads 'Doeg & Arnold, Auctioneer & estate agents'.

The building's opening on 31 July 1890 was celebrated with a banquet organised by the owner, Mrs Elizabeth Delaney. The original occupants included about thirty shops along with a Turkish bathhouse, billiard rooms, a restaurant, an oyster saloon and the splendid Arcade Club Hotel. Mrs Delaney would have looked forward to a prosperous future. Turkish baths were popular in Melbourne at the time: there were at least ten others, including one in the Royal Arcade, and the City Baths, which closed as recently as

1983. A number of charming, carefully painted ghost signs on one of the entrances, giving further details of the occupants, have been uncovered and protected behind screens.

But Mrs Delaney's timing was poor. In 1890, Melbourne was entering a long recession – one of our usual busts brought about by rampant property speculation. Banks closed, businesses went to the wall, unemployment spiralled. Mrs Delaney lost control of the arcade, whose ownership passed to The Caledonian and Australian Finance Agency, and the architect was declared insolvent. Thereafter, the arcade took on a different life. During the early twentieth century it was occupied by organisations such as the Theosophical Society, the Independent Workers' Union and the Melbourne and Suburban Fuel Men's Association. In the 1920s, renamed The Centreway – a name still visible in an entrance mosaic – it was home to the Centreway Disposals Co, Eterna Shirts and Blue Jay Manufacturing. By then, the era of arcades had passed, and department stores were the new big thing. A photograph of the interior taken in the 1950s shows it as a rather lonely, depressing place.

In the 1960s it became Dan Murphys, occupying the whole ground floor for several decades, and bringing the arcade to life again. In those days, Dan Murphy himself ran the place, and began teaching a generation of Melburnians about wine. Around the same time, the upper storeys of the arcade took on another lease of life as the home of artists and musicians. Howard Arkley, the great documenter of Melbourne suburbia, had a studio here, in a building as architecturally different as could be imagined from the humble suburban houses he immortalised in his work. From 1992 to 1998 Lindsay Gravina operated the Birdland recording studio on the first floor, producing 'the most important records of the 90s' with bands like The Living End, Cosmic Psychos, Magic Dirt and Spiderbait. He recalls: 'I lived there with no shower or hot running water and hosted a constantly changing coterie of outsiders – musicians, painters, writers and just straight up weirdos. There were hundreds of crazy parties that spilled out onto the balcony and sometimes the roof! But it was the never ending parade of fascinating characters that the building seemed to attract which made that place very special.'

In the 1980s the National Trust carried out a survey of the building, concluding: 'The Prahran Arcade is one of the three most significant arcades in Victoria, and probably the second most architecturally significant' (after The Block Arcade). However, it was never very successful as an arcade, its shops offering few of the glamorous luxury items that bourgeois shoppers craved. Looked at in that way, it was a failure. On the other hand, it played an important part in suburban life as the home of retailers, community organisations, musicians and artists, and that gives it a special place in Melbourne's social history. And, like other examples of bonkers late Victoriana, it retains its capacity to astonish. The distressed state of the building only adds to its romantic allure, as it snoozes on Chapel Street, a place of strange beauty for those who raise their eyes and take a moment to appreciate its uniqueness. Who knows ... perhaps one day the small shops will return, and the arcade will once again echo with the feet of flaneurs strolling from Turkish bath to oyster saloon.

MOSHIACH IS COMING!

We fled to East St Kilda in the early 1990s, refugees from the outer eastern suburbs. Our first residence in Melbourne was the house where you'd grown up, from the age of fifteen or so anyway, in Blackburn South. Your mum still lived there, your dad had left years ago, and neither you nor your siblings had fond memories of that house. Still, your mum made us welcome there for a few months in 1990, while we got our act together. Soon enough, we found our own place, a tiny flat, sans furniture, in nearby Burwood. The neighbourhood was a cultural Gobi: our only entertainment was a stroll along the Burwood Highway to the 7-Eleven, reminding you of the soul-destroying emptiness of your teenage years. Our neighbour was a young bloke called Todd whose major interest was revving the engine of his car by day and night. 'Throbbing Todd' you called him. Despite being just off a suburban highway, the place had a bit of greenery, and we walked down its concrete steps to the smell of gum trees. The flat was invaded regularly by huntsman spiders – hairy saucer-sized fuckers that scuttled across our pillows at night. We needed to get away from Throbbing Todd and the Huntsmen (not unlike the kind of bands that performed at the nearby Burvale Hotel), and our next stop was East St Kilda.

The pad on Alma Place belonged to friends of a friend. They were middle-class hippies who had gone to India to live on an ashram, clearing out of their nicely furnished house for a year. It sounded pretty dodgy, as the ashram was under the auspices of Rajneesh, the shyster mystic and sex guru, and owner of a fleet of Rolls Royces, who was busted in the 1980s for the usual suite of tax fraud and sex offences. The house was full of books of vacuous 'philosophy' with his crooked bearded visage on the cover. The thing you found most hilarious about the ashram was that the residents played a form of nude consciousness-raising tennis called 'zennis'. Anyway, we lived in their house for a year or so, and even slept on their waterbed, which sloshed and slurped weirdly beneath us, perhaps in homage to one of the guru's helpful axioms: 'Do not swim – float!'

The house was long and thin, with a long thin garden at the back, in which we daringly had open-air sex once or twice, as if in our own ashram. The guys next door were less discreet: sounds of loud shagging emanated at full volume through their open windows every night. There was a mouse infestation that year: one ate poison at our neighbours' place and came to die in our hallway. We chased him onto the road where he was squelched by a truck at a spot we referred to forever after as 'Flatmouse Corner'. We went to movies at The Astor, where we saw a lot of Hitchcock and Scorsese and Truffaut and Capra. Yothu Yindi, Dave Graney, Paul Kelly and Frente played at festivals on the foreshore. We ate at the Galleon, the legendary café on Carlisle Street where you always had spanakopita and salad followed by kugelhopf. (The Galleon's name harks back to an older institution, Ye Kynges Galleone on Acland Street, a popular jazz club, whose name I spotted in our 1946 Sands & McDougall.)

Acland Street was thriving back then, filled with endlessly interesting offerings: Cosmos, the book and record shop; numerous cake shops; Sheherazade's café; and a cool little second-hand book cave around the corner in Barkley Street (now a supermarket). Once someone jemmied open the back door of our house and robbed us, taking some of your jewellery, a CD player, and my camera. The ashramites' large television was left behind, as was their collection of books on tantric transformation, the burglar resisting the opportunity for spiritual improvement. The cops told us: 'If they want to get in, they'll get in. It doesn't matter what precautions you take. That's the price of living in St Kilda.' We thought of Burwood, looked at each other and shrugged. We wanted to live in St Kilda.

There was a Thai restaurant on the Nepean Highway, just five minutes away. Thai was in vogue in the early 90s, and we felt quite sophisticated eating there. One night, our waiter was a young guy who joyfully recognised you from Wodonga High School, where he'd been a student when you were a first-year teacher. You remembered him too, a gay kid who'd been bullied and had made his escape to the big city. It was the first occurrence of what subsequently happened a lot during our time together, when you would run into someone you used to teach in Wodonga or Melbourne. After you died, I kept finding cards that students had given you, dozens of them, with messages of hope and thanks: 'Now I can fly with my own wings'. They must be all over the city and beyond, those people whose lives you touched, bits of language in their heads that you taught them, diplomas on their walls that you guided them towards. I'm conscious that I share you with them, that you loved them, and you are still with them as you are with me.

Our second place in East St Kilda was a post-war flat on Mooltan Avenue, just off Hotham Street. It was the heart of the Ashkenazi community, and many of its occupants were elderly: the sounds of opera boomed from their windows rather than vigorous sex. We haunted Balaclava's cafés and delis, weaving around the men in dark suits, hats and beards. Among the locals were followers of the Moshiach, a New York rabbi said by some to be the Messiah: his hairy face adorned billboards at the intersection of Dandenong Road and Chapel Street, with the words 'MOSHIACH IS COMING!' First Rajneesh, now Moshiach: we were being stalked by bearded mystics.

It was 1993, the year we decided to get married: also the year that Paul Keating pulled off the impossible election victory. We turned on the telly at the precise moment he famously announced 'this was a victory for the true believers' and hugged each other with incredulous delight. The following year, we had our Australian wedding in St Kilda Botanical Gardens. It was a wet and blustery day, so we had to wait for a break in the weather to say our vows, and as the celebrant had another event soon afterwards she delivered her lines at speed, all but running out of the gate as she said 'husband and wife' over her shoulder: we dubbed her The Galloping Celebrant.

Although we were only in East St Kilda a couple of years, they were important times. We were learning to be together in the ordinary day-to-dayness, laying down our store of shared memories, jokes and mythologies, like images painted onto a wall. Twenty-five years later, we could look at each other and say, 'Remember Flatmouse Corner?' or 'Anyone for zennis?' or 'I wonder where the Galloping Celebrant is now?' Now that you've gone, I have these jokes to myself, though I still sometimes say them to you, in the quiet of our room or out on the street, when I sense you nudging me as a white-bearded old man approaches: Moshiach is coming!

THREE WOMEN OF ST KILDA CEMETERY

Twenty or more years ago, when we lived in East St Kilda, we occasionally visited the cemetery on Hotham Street. It's one of Melbourne's oldest, established in the 1850s, and there are few new interments here: perhaps for this reason, one seldom sees other visitors. We revisit the cemetery while psychojogging, and are struck by the different ways that people choose to remember their dead.

Many old graves use the same euphemisms. The words *darling wife, loving daughter, cherished father, fell asleep, called home, departed this life, regretted, sadly missed* are fading to illegibility on weathered, sometime toppled headstones. *Fell asleep ... called home* ... what use are such euphemisms? Some resort to more flowery, or creepy, clichés: *Another bud to bloom in heaven. God's finger touched him and he slept.* As is the way in cemeteries, many graves are long abandoned, weed-infested, the stone cracked or broken, listing like ships in a storm. Some are completely shattered. There's a sadness about these graves: are their occupants completely forgotten? Other graves are well maintained, a very few have fresh flowers or something more poignant: a child's grave is adorned with Thomas the Tank Engine toys. A sea captain's has a stone anchor and chain; a soldier's, a slouch hat; a memorial to a member of the Fire Brigade, metal taps and shields bearing helmets.

Among the dead, we find familiar names. Here's Dame Mabel Brookes, the Melbourne society leader and writer whom we first came across at the Maribyrnong Explosives Factory. Walking through South Yarra, we bumped into her again at 'Raveloe', the family home described in her memoirs as 'the place of many parties and much fun and carefree youth'. Our paths cross for the last time in St Kilda cemetery, where Mabel Brookes and her husband share a headstone. Along with the dates, their titles are listed:

NORMAN EVERARD BROOKES
KNIGHT BACHELOR, CHEV. LEG. D'HONNEUR
MABEL BALCOMBE BROOKES
C.B.E., D.B.E.
CHEV. LEG. D'HONNEUR, L.L.D. HON.

That impressive collection of titles and honours acknowledges considerable charity work, in particular her years as president of the Queen Victoria Hospital. The French honour arose from a startling family connection with the island of St Helena, a remote Atlantic island where Napoleon had been exiled after his defeat at Waterloo. Norman and Mabel presented the French government with the pavilion Napoleon had occupied, which was on an estate Mabel's family owned in St Helena. They received France's top honour in return, as you do. Surprisingly, no mention is made here of Sir Norman's tennis achievements, though he was the first Australian winner of Wimbledon and a world number 1: giving a bit of real estate to the French government was apparently more significant.

Not far from their grave is that of artist Sybil Craig (1901–1989), who also turned up at the Maribyrnong Explosives Factory, where she was an official war artist. She shares a plot with her parents and the gravestone bears only their names and the words 'At rest'. Craig spent almost all her life in Melbourne, living in the same house, first with her parents and then alone after their death. She's the opposite of Dr King, the shape-shifting, globe-trotting quack doctor whose life epitomised his time: her life followed a safe, predictable path. Living in one place all your life can give you a sense of connectedness: on the other hand, it's somewhat limiting. Yet her wartime paintings imply a different spirit: experimental, energetic and curious. Biographers say there were other works, more experimental, which she never showed publicly. Would a different city have brought them out of her? Did staid old Melbourne hold her back?

– I wonder if she ever longed to escape ...

Our attention is caught by a memorial on a much larger scale: a marble statue of a woman seated on a tomb between four pillars. Despite the size, it is not for anyone famous, but 'in loving memory' of a young woman named Doleen Maude LaBarte. Who was she, and why was she commemorated in this way? According to the cemetery's information booklet, she was a 'murder victim'. The events of her death in 1920 attracted sensational media coverage all over the country, with the inquest and the trial unfolding before packed courtrooms, so the details are easy to find.

Doleen LaBarte was born at roughly the same time as Mabel Brookes and Sybil Craig, and like them came from a well-off Melbourne family, being the daughter of a solicitor. The recently married Doleen was killed in Moss Vale, New South Wales by her husband Major Thomas LaBarte, a war veteran who had served in France. They had been married for little more than a year when he shot her sixteen times. LaBarte also killed a policeman, Constable Frederick Mitchell, at the scene, then telephoned the police to announce, 'I have shot one policeman, and I will shoot them all'. A siege took place before LaBarte was arrested.

When put on trial, La Barte claimed that he could not remember anything that had happened. In words depressingly familiar in domestic violence cases then as now, he said that his wife was the dearest person in the world to him, and he would not have done her any harm. Due to La Barte's status as a war hero, the case attracted publicity across the country and was heard before the Chief Justice of New South Wales. La Barte's defence was that he was suffering from 'war strain' and was temporarily insane when he killed his wife. Expert witnesses agreed.

> Dr. William A. Morton (V.), said he had been for several years in France as a medical officer with the A.I.F. His experience showed that the nervous system was greatly affected by war strain, especially in cases where men were blown up by high explosives. Sometimes the trouble took the form of acute mania. He had seen a good deal of accused after the major's return from the front. LaBarte, who appeared to be suffering very much from war strain, was nervous and restless, and had a tremor in his hands. He was not then drinking. Witness was not surprised when he read of the tragedy.
> – *The Register* (Adelaide) 6 April 1921.

The jury accepted the defence and returned a verdict of manslaughter, so LaBarte escaped the death penalty for both killings. The press dubbed him 'the demented major'.

In their grief, Doleen La Barte's family erected a memorial that dwarfs that of the prime minister and architect of Federation, Alfred Deakin, who with his wife Pattie is buried nearby in a very simple grave. In time, other family members of Doleen were buried with her in the family tomb. Was it a public demonstration of the depth of their feelings? Or perhaps a rebuke to society for giving all the attention to Major La Barte? As is still the case today, the courts and media focussed on the perpetrator, not the victim. The papers reported the details of his life (war service et cetera), but hers was largely disregarded. Maybe the tomb was a place the family came to remember her. But for all its scale, the tomb is impersonal: it tells us nothing about the person Doleen LaBarte was. Instead, it communicates the feelings of the bereaved.

I get it, though. In grief, we act for reasons we don't understand. We try to make sense of events that are senseless. We have to do *something*. The funeral of Sir Frederick Sargood, another politician and businessman buried here, had 'eight massed bands, 1200 cadets and a firing party of 300. Members of the Metropolitan Liedertafel sang Sullivan's 'The Long Day Closes'.' What is the best way to remember someone we have lost? Some people set up foundations. Run marathons, climb mountains. Take up a cause. Raise funds for a hospital. Write a song. Find some way to derive meaning from what has happened. *God's finger touched him and he slept*. Does any of that, in the end, make us feel any better? Is that even the point? I'm certain a marble monument to you would be of no comfort to me. But it's as well not to judge what anyone else does in these situations. Joan Didion writes, 'Grief turns out to be a place none of us know until we reach it.' We make our own ways of remembering, like that guy and his beer under the West Gate Bridge. Maybe this book is mine.

CITY OF BOOKS

The Beatles can be found in Narre Warren, where the Strawberry Fields estate includes street names such as Lennon Court and Ringo Place; a team of cricketers inhabits Keilor East, and Arthurian legends abound in Glen Waverley. In Maidstone, we encountered a squadron of flying aces around the old RAAF base. Such 'clusters' of street names are a phenomenon of suburbia. We come across another in Elwood, where we enter the city of books. The streets are named after poets and novelists, many of them English – Shelley, Wordsworth, Dickens, Byron – joined by a couple of Australians, Lawson and Lindsay. The names feel appropriate because the whole suburb has a romantic, fictional atmosphere. There's an other-worldly atmosphere about these streets, which are dotted with houses and apartment buildings in a bewildering range of styles. The houses have names like 'Camelot Court', 'Avalon', 'Montmar', 'De Montrose', 'La Casita', 'Dynevor Court', and 'Juliette'

(probably not named after Sade's murderous heroine, but who knows what goes on in there?). On Tennyson Avenue, among the houses we spot 'Merlin', 'Godiva', and 'Vivien', all characters in Tennyson's Arthurian poetry. Will wily Vivien appear on one of those balconies, ready to lure Merlin up that staircase?

Nearby, traces of a more mundane past linger. Close to Elwood junction, at 16 Ormond Road, we can faintly make out a ghost sign that reads 'The Elwood Confectioner'. My Sands & McDougall places C.A. Winterburn, confectioner, here in 1946, and perhaps the shop was a confectioner's for many years on either side of that date. Jerry's café on Barkly Street is adorned with uniquely Melburnian signage: ghost signs for Robur Tea, Swallow and Ariell biscuits, and *The Age* which comes 'fresh daily'. There's another 'Confectionery' sign across the top, and the word 'PILLS' (perhaps a further manifestation of Dr Morse, whose Indian Root Pills we have seen advertised throughout the city) lurks below the Swallows sign. Ordinary as they are, time has lent these old signs a patina of romance.

Back in the land of the poets, it's startling to be confronted by a Victorian mansion at 14 Hennessy Avenue. Named Sherwood Hall, a name that evokes Robin Hood (another legendary figure of Olde England), it is flats today. We wander around, take some photos, and speculate on its history. What local big shot might have built it? What fate befell him?

The answer, when we delve into the history of the place with help from the National Trust, turns out to be worthy of a Dickens novel. The house, originally named Rothermere (or Rotherfield – both names turn up, confusingly) was built in 1891 for Joseph Cowen Syme, the nephew of David Syme, proprietor and editor of *The Age*. A shrewd businessman and political operator, David published the newspaper 'fresh daily' for half a century. Young Joseph, described as a 'forceful character' – and you can imagine what Dickens would have done with that – was a partner in *The Age* for a few years. But David didn't much like sharing control with anyone, and the stormy partnership ended with David buying out his nephew's share of the business for £140,000. Displaying the usual modesty of media magnates, Joseph used the money to finance this 45-room mansion, designed by David Askew and built by Thomas Machin. Joseph, who apparently didn't rate highly for interpersonal skills, fell out with Machin too, and was successfully sued when he didn't pay for the job.

But Joseph lived in the house until he died in 1916, and his widow Laura rattled around in the forty-five rooms until her own death, again in a style worthy of Dickens. In the late 1920s, like many mansions around this part of town and across Melbourne, the building was converted to a guest house and subsequently flats. The estate was subdivided, after which most of the houses and apartment blocks on Hennessy and Wimbledon Avenues were built.

Looking at Syme's mansion, it strikes us that the house might more appropriately be located on nearby Shelley Street. It was the radical Shelley who in his poem 'Ozymandias' debunked the pretensions of the rich and powerful, with their 'sneer of cold command'. 'Look on my Works, ye Mighty, and despair! Nothing beside remains.' Unlike the shattered remains of Ozymandias's statue, and many grandiose Melbourne mansions built by over-reaching businessmen, something at least does remain of Rothermere/Rotherfield, whether you consider it an example of fine architecture or a symbol of self-importance.

As we wander these broad quiet streets, beneath the spreading boughs of plane trees and ankle-deep in autumn leaves, it seems that that if we had been dropped at random here from a passing aeroplane it would be hard to know quite where in the world we were. The streetscape has been put together as if by someone assembling an all-purpose stage set for costume dramas – there's Spanish mission, art deco, mock Tudor, art nouveau, Victorian and more. Are there hidden cameras somewhere? Have we ourselves become characters in a drama? We couldn't afford to live here these days, now that it's one of Melbourne's most desirable suburbs, all cafes and trendy wine shops, and so close to the beach. Still we can wander and wonder, imagining the narratives that might unfold.

*

We were both lifelong wanderers in the city of books. By and large, we followed our own paths through that city, but they intersected at various points. You'd journeyed through the French Quarter when you were a student, accumulating that shelf of yellow-spined French classics by La Bruyere, Laclos, Diderot, Stendhal, Flaubert, Sartre, and Camus that I still possess. Most have Melbourne University Bookroom price labels on the cover. Your name is neatly written on the flyleaf, and details of classes that you'd jotted down: '10 am–12, 16 October, Room 518'. Sometimes you wrote lecture and vocabulary notes inside, in your handwriting that never changed all the years I knew you: I'd recognise it anywhere. You've left little traces of yourself all over these books, and I study them now, hoping to catch a glimpse of you or to hear your voice. Occasionally there's a bit of paper or a tram ticket; two dry dead leaves flutter out of *Madame Bovary*, thinner than tissue paper. From where, and why? I'll never know, but they meant something to you once, and I'm glad to have them. These echoes of the past call to me across time and I imagine you sitting in some lecture hall or library, frowning over your book. I picture you as a 24-year old on the Swanston Street tram to uni, holding onto the pole, book in hand, or seated by the window, immersed in a novel, frowning slightly, one finger twirling your hair.

You hadn't read them all, of course. Some had been gathered almost at random from second-hand shops, a habit all book lovers have (I'm the same, or worse). For example, that thin French book titled *Le Jansénisme* which you inexplicably bought on a whim one day. Jansénism was a particularly grim and charmless form of you're-all-going-to-hell Christianity, which couldn't have been further from your own outlook: perhaps it had come up in a history lecture. Anyway, you never read it, but even after thirty years, you refused to consider getting rid of the book. I used to tease you about it.

> *– 'Tell me about Le Jansénisme,' I'd insist.*
> *– 'No, it would go over your head.'*
> *– 'Just the main points.'*
> *– 'I can't summarise it. The effect on me was too profound…'*
> *and so on.*

The French writer whose work you enjoyed most was Georges Simenon. You loved Inspector Maigret, doggedly solving murders then going home to his mundane domestic life: a philosophical, ordinary man just getting on with things. By the time I met you, though, you'd moved past those books. You'd taught French in Wodonga, spent a year in France as an *assistante d'Anglais* in a high school, and had lived in Barcelona for a year. We met shortly after that, when we were teaching English to recalcitrant European teenagers during the unusually long hot English summer of 1988. The place: Reading. I was there because I was newly qualified and it was the first job that came up: you were there because you'd read Oscar Wilde's *Ballad of Reading Gaol* and wanted to see the city for yourself. So we met because of Oscar in a way, but I don't remember many conversations about books during those hilarious drunken evenings. That came later, when we were living on separate continents, you in Egypt, me in Italy, and we exchanged long letters via air mail. 'We read to know we are not alone,' according to C.S. Lewis, but those who read generally like to find others who also read, so that they can be not-alone together.

We discovered, via correspondence, a connection that would last the rest of our lives. It wasn't that we always agreed: in fact, when we disagreed, as over your taste for the peyote-crazed novels of Tom Robbins, you refuted my criticisms with a fervour I found more attractive than agreement. When we moved to Australia together, you were my guide to that region of the city of books, where I encountered Henry Lawson, Banjo Paterson, Ruth Park, Katharine Susannah Prichard, Martin Boyd, Judith Wright, Helen Garner. During our first trip to Sydney together, revisiting your childhood haunts, we met an old bloke near The Rocks who claimed to be Lawson's nephew. We weren't sure whether to believe him, but he looked and sounded the part, a shabby unreliable narrator with a good spiel – just like a character in one of 'Uncle' Henry's stories – so we decided to take him at his word, and he became part of our history, a distant connection with one of our heroes from the city of books.

Later came your Fitzgeralds jag. There wouldn't be a biography of Zelda, Scott or anyone connected with them – kids, friends, editors – that you didn't read. You even got hold of Zelda's novel, *Save Me the Waltz*, published posthumously in 1953. What fascinated you about her, besides the fact that she was obviously brilliant and glamorous and doomed, was that it was Scott who was hailed as the genius, while for you theirs was a partnership, dysfunctional though it was much of the time. So hers was a story about how a talented spirited young woman struggles to achieve something important in the world despite the forces holding her back.

Something similar was at work in your favourite novel, *Portrait of a Lady*, Henry James's great story of 'a certain young woman affronting her destiny', which you must have read half a dozen times, and were still reading until a few months before you died, when your eyes gave out (one of the cruellest things about that disease was that it robbed you of reading) and you turned to me one night and said, 'I've finally figured out why I love this book so much, it explains it all ...' And you told me about Isabel Archer's struggle to live independently and travel and find love, despite the people plotting around her, and the subtle, brutal way James describes the moment when, detecting a single glance between Osmond and Madame Merle, Isabel understands how she has been deceived. That novel, of the thousands of books you consumed in a lifetime of reading, spoke most deeply to you about the complexities and hazards of a woman's life.

After you died I had to do a bit of sorting out, and I chose not to keep everything, but there are several shelves of things I'll hold on to. The city of books is vast, and no one visits more than a fraction of it, but you took me places I'd never have seen otherwise, and as with urban wandering, you see more in the company of other travellers. So I have kept the shelf of French classics, and Maigret, and Zelda, and *Portrait of a Lady*. And I even kept the unread *Le Jansénisme*, not because I care about that grim and humourless sect, but because, perhaps inappropriately, it still makes me laugh.

THE LOST NAMES OF EMERALD HILL

A wave of Irish migration brought your family from Enniskillen to Sydney in the 1920s. Your surname is well known in Ireland: it's a famous liqueur consisting of whiskey and cream. You have a swag of Irish rellies all over the globe. And one of your distant ancestors was a celebrated harpist and composer – Turlough O'Carolan – whose music is still performed today. He wandered Ireland finding rich patrons, in exchange for which he'd write music to pay for his keep. You still have distant cousins there, whom you visited in your 20s on your first overseas trip, looking for a connection, like many young Australians. They fed you potatoes cooked four different ways, although it's a vegetable you've never liked. You often recounted the scene to me, familiar to anyone who knows Irish hospitality:

> – *Sure and you'll have a wee bit more mash.*
> – *Thank you but ...*
> – *Just a few more chips now.*
> – *Well actually ...*
> – *I'll just give you another baked potato.* And the plate was piled high again.

Your nanna in Sydney kept her Irish accent all her life, and was quite clear where her loyalties lay. 'Don't have anything to do with those English blackguards,' she impressed on you when you were a child, advice you liked to remind me of when we had a disagreement. While you loved most of your relatives, you were ambivalent about your ancestry. There was pain and rage there as well as love, and the origins of your family's hurt could be traced past your childhood in Sydney's western suburbs, and back across the Atlantic to Enniskillen. Every family is as complex as a city, every history is personal and contested, and ghost signs of trauma linger from one generation to the next.

We talked about this as our walk took us into South Melbourne, near the corner of Montague Street and Bank Street, where the former Shannon and Shamrock Hotel stands, a reminder of the days when Melbourne had Irish pubs, rather than Irish-themed pubs. Many Irish migrants were influential in the hotel trade, and around South Melbourne, one can still visit the Limerick Arms on Clarendon Street and O'Connells (these days a 'stylish gastropub') on Coventry Street. The Irish also worked on the docks, slaking their thirst at the dockside pubs. As we know, the 'celebrated specialist', Dr King, was Irish; perhaps Mrs Delaney of the Prahran Arcade was too. The Shannon and Shamrock hasn't been an operating hotel since the 1920s – these days it is offices – but you can still see the name rendered at the top of the building, and ghost signs at ground floor level. We stand looking up at the old signage, and to you it doesn't just represent an old pub: behind it you can see the history of a wave of migration.

Beside the Shamrock is a smaller building once occupied by Frank Cullen, plumber. With a name like that he was probably Irish too, and the name is faintly visible in black and white lettering. The business was established in 1894, so says the sign, but Cullen was still here in 1946, according to Sands & McDougall. He was licensed by M.M.B.W. (the Melbourne Metropolitan Board of Works), a long-gone authority responsible for water and sanitation, and his phone number was MX2436. MX represents the telephone exchange, and four digits were the norm for phone numbers in the 1940s. Like the lost postcodes, the old telephone exchanges are a forgotten classification system. There were thousands across the state of Victoria, some of which only had one line: but in the metropolitan area, South Melbourne was one of the largest, along with Brighton, Carlton, Collingwood, Footscray and Central.

Lost numbers, lost names: Melbourne has books full of them. There are names that appeared on old maps then dropped into disuse. The Maribyrnong River was once the Saltwater. The area around Flagstaff Gardens used to be Batman's Hill. (Given Batman's murderous history, perhaps it's time to stop naming anything after him.) In the nineteenth century, South Melbourne was more poetically referred to as Emerald Hill. There are many lost names to be seen on its walls today, as we've seen during this walk: they are an archive of people, occupations, products, social movements.

We continue east along Bank Street, passing Victorian terraces, solid red-brick Victorian buildings, and Housing Commission flats on our right. Reaching the corner of Cecil and Bank Streets, we come across a Victorian corner shop with quaint signage. As we stand there admiring it, a wedding party (plus photographer) turns up, keen to commemorate their special day in the company of Dr Scott's Balsam Horehound, Marchall's Rhubarb Pills for the liver (useful if you've over-indulged at the Shamrock Hotel), and J.J. King's self-raising flour. The prices – three pence (3d) and six pence (6d) are prominently displayed. Given the age of the building, along with the products and the style of the signwriting, these signs could be from the 1880s or 1890s.

Dr Scott's Balsam Horehound is another addition to our collection of lost doctors and medicines: in North Carlton we came across Otis Tonic Tablets on the rear wall of an old pharmacy; in North Melbourne and Elwood we encountered Dr Morse's Indian Root Pills; and in Russell Street we met Dr King. We often wonder how real any of Melbourne's long-dead doctors were. In the case of Dr King, he certainly existed, although his profession of 'medical clairvoyant' was open to question. Dr Morse was a fiction dreamed up by an advertising team. And Dr Scott? I have no idea, but it's still possible to buy antique bottles of Balsam Horehound online.

Then there are the lost social movements. Take the Temperance Hall on Napier Street, one of many which sprouted all over Melbourne in the late nineteenth century, built by the movement opposed to alcohol and its malign influence. (The first we ever saw was the Yarra Coffee Palace in Yarraville.) Given the number of pubs in South Melbourne, it's safe to say that temperance was seldom in the ascendant here, and we can guess that the social consequences of alcohol were prominent too. Converted into a theatre space in the 1980s that is still used for performances, the hall was an important gathering place for those who wanted a sober evening out.

More evidence of friendly societies can be found on Coventry Street, where the UFS (United Friendly Societies) dispensary still displays its signage. Friendly societies were co-operatives of members who supported each other in various ways. They had marvellous names like Foresters, Free Gardeners, Oddfellows and Rechabites, also gone from our twentieth century vocabulary, although you can find their names on walls around the suburbs. Some, like the Rechabites, were active in the temperance movement. The quirky names shouldn't obscure the valuable work they did, which included providing insurance and benefits schemes as well as dispensaries. Now that healthcare, workplace insurance and pensions are largely the responsibility of governments, we don't need friendly societies to provide them, although the descendants of some survive as large financial institutions, their names harking back to alternative forms of social organisation.

There seems no end to the lost names that linger around South Melbourne: insurance companies, estate agents, outfitters, newspapers. On Dorcas Street, we spot the offices of two lost newspapers, *The Courier* and *The Record*, in which our friend Dr James King placed his 'beware of barefaced imposters!' notice. One can imagine reporters in brown hats rushing out of the door, notebook in hand, heading for a nearby fire or robbery. On the same street, we notice the signage of McCauleys furniture store dating from the early twentieth century. Once the business occupied a whole block between Mitchell and Clarendon streets before it abruptly disappeared from the street directory in 1935. Nevertheless, the signage remains, along with a human hand, directing passers-by to a shop that no longer exists.

But the most interesting collection of lost names is hidden down Raglan Street, where we come across a mysterious Victorian building behind iron railings and a neat garden. The words 'SEE YUP' appear in red Victorian lettering above the gates. Moving closer, we realise that, despite the building's western classical architecture, it is a Chinese temple. At the entrance are stone lions, flowers, and Chinese inscriptions. Inside – where photography is not allowed but anyone can wander around – are hundreds of candles, red lanterns, Chinese script on the columns, fruit piled high on altars, and the aroma of incense.

The See Yup Temple was built in 1866, financed by discoveries on the goldfields by Chinese diggers, many of whom came from the See Yup districts of Guangdong. The See Yup Society was a mutual self-help organisation for Chinese migrants, not unlike those quaintly-named friendly societies. With its fine architecture and splendid interior, the temple symbolised the success of the Chinese community on the goldfields. It was, and is, a centre of worship, as well as a death registry containing thousands of memorial tablets with the names and home districts of society members who died in Victoria. Dating back one-and-a-half centuries, the tablets preserve the details of the Chinese diggers who came to Victoria during the Gold Rush, and their many successors. The temple is a house of memory, immortalising thousands of names that would otherwise be lost to oblivion.

During the first half of the twentieth century, the Chinese population of Melbourne decreased, due largely to racism given official form by anti-Chinese policies of immigration and employment. Nevertheless, Chinese people continued to make a living in occupations such as market gardening and laundries. The temple was in decline by the 1930s, and by the 1960s it had fallen into a state of disrepair: the building had been vandalised, the windows boarded up, and the gardens were a wilderness. During that time, it seemed likely that the building would be sold or demolished. (After our visit, I look through the National Trust archives where I come across an article featuring an image of a young Barry Humphries, lounging on a lion, and cheekily claiming that he wanted to buy the temple.)

Fortunately, neither the sale nor the demolition eventuated. As Chinese migration increased again, there was renewed interest in the temple. In the 1970s it was restored by the Chinese community with the support of the National Trust, and partly financed by government grants. More recently, another grant enabled the 13,000 memorial tablets to be cleaned and restored, and the inscriptions entered into a database. The lost names of the See Yup temple have thus found a new home in cyberspace.

I've been calling them 'lost names', but they are not yet totally lost. The desire to hold on is profound, whether it's by painting a name, erecting a statue, or collecting stone tablets. I try to do it in words: I've filled pages with memories, albums with photos. But it's an unachievable goal. Even statues crumble, paintings fade, ghost signs weather away to a blank wall, as will the poignant mural on the Grand Theatre in Footscray. The man reaches out to grab his lover who is slipping away, but she is always just out of reach, and in time they will both melt into nothingness. Joan Didion writes in *The Year of Magical Thinking,* her memoir about the death of her husband: 'The apprehension that our life together will decreasingly be the centre of my every day seemed today on Lexington Avenue so distinct a betrayal that I lost all sense of oncoming traffic.'

But something remains, as long as there is someone to remember: memories of a gesture, a word, a smile, as when one turns a corner and comes across a faded sign, a pointing hand. In these moments the past is present, and you are next to me again.

DREAM HOUSES PAST AND PRESENT

We've become used to typical streetscapes in Melbourne: rows of small Victorian cottages, red brick Federation houses in established suburbs, clusters of oversized mansions in newer developments, hip architect-designed boxes, weatherboards, and the Housing Commission towers that punctuate the city like exclamation marks. Most of it is pretty familiar after a while. But heading east from Graham Street and south of Williamstown Road in Port Melbourne we come across streets like none we have seen before – at least, not in this city. It feels as if we have stumbled through some time-and-travel machine into a British housing estate. (The fact that it is raining as we walk probably adds to the illusion.) In fact, it is a social experiment from the 1920s.

The uniformity of the streetscape strikes us first – street after street of large two-storey semi-detached houses, with some variations but very similar in their fundamentals. Another thing we notice is how un-Melbourne-like they look. Instead of the familiar small workers' cottages with service lanes running up the back, or the larger brick Edwardian houses favoured by the middle classes, these are all semi-detached. There's no brick or weatherboard in sight; they are built of concrete blocks with cement render, and have a solid, austere look. The streets are lined with trees, and there are reserves where you can stroll among native trees, watch your kids on the playground, or even have a hit of trugo.

We have wandered into Garden City, an interwar experiment in social planning, described at the time as 'the dream city of Fishermens Bend'.

Built and financed by the Victorian State Savings Bank, the houses were always owner-occupied. When construction began in 1926, Melbourne was experiencing a severe housing shortage, and unemployment was high, soon to become even worse when the Depression hit. At roughly the same time, a few suburbs away, maverick architect Howard Lawson was creating his fantastical apartment buildings. There was an obvious need for low-cost housing options, but rather than embark on a large-scale project of its own, the government outsourced the job to the State Bank, which took the job seriously: the general manager went on a tour of Britain, looking for low-cost housing options. The plan was to develop a 'garden city' modelled on the ideas of Ebenezer Howard, author of the influential *Garden Cities of Tomorrow*. Howard advocated affordable, solid housing in pleasant surroundings, amid parks and gardens, where ordinary people could enjoy healthy conditions instead of slums.

In Jane Jacobs's *The Death and Life of Great American Cities*, Jacobs trashes Howard and his thinking as paternalist and at odds with how cities actually work. Instead of creating diverse urban spaces, Jacobs argues, with shops and bars and factories and houses all mingled together, Howard and his disciples wanted to separate the houses from everything else. This killed the experience of urban life, she wrote, because no one was ever on the streets. That criticism could probably be aimed at many of Melbourne's suburbs, garden cities or not, but the people who lived in these houses in Port Melbourne seemed pretty happy with them. Jean Johnson, who moved into Poolman Street in 1927, declared: 'I'm so delighted with our new home! There's no need to go outside for anything and no detail that makes for comfort and convenience has been omitted. There is even a linen press tucked under the stairs!'

In the end, there were 322 'bank houses' in Garden City, created in six different designs, which alternate as we walk along the street. However, at £1000 each, they were not exactly houses for the poor as they were more expensive than the average house. The Garden's underpinning ideology favoured home-ownership over renting and there wasn't much chance of a working-class family buying one of these properties. Hence, Garden City became known as 'Nob's Hill', a sharp contrast to the nearby Housing Commission estate built later on when the government decided to build large-scale welfare housing.

These days there are strict rules about what modications Garden City homeowners can and cannot make to their properties. This results in a uniform streetscape quite unlike the hodge-podge that you find in many suburbs. Whether you think uniform = boring is a matter of personal taste I suppose, but the external state of these houses is quite rigorously policed, although owners have more freedom to make changes on the inside. The Garden City Guidelines in 1997 ominously reprimanded: 'additions have been made including bay windows, window shutters, planter boxes, pergolas, balconies and garages ... unsympathetic modifications like these are slowly but surely undermining the integrity of the area.' First, they came for our planter boxes ...

Garden City is an interesting pocket utopia, an attempt at social planning which does not seem to have been widely emulated (not in Melbourne, anyway). Walking around it, we wonder at the lack of shops, milk bars, pubs. We have always appreciated the fact that there is a strip of shops and a primary school at the end of our street in Yarraville. But judging by current house prices, there is still a lot of interest in living here: we'd need well over a million to buy one of these houses now.

In Melbourne, home-owners tend to resist the idea that

streetscapes should be uniform. The suburbs are a weird mixture of architecture, often in complete disharmony: personal choice is everything, whether or not it matches anyone else's choices. Our own little weatherboard in the Parish of Cut Paw Paw is gradually being surrounded by houses completely out of sync with the original streetscape in style and scale. Other cities, such as Montreal, take a more regulated approach, resulting in streetscapes that have small variations within an aesthetically pleasing uniformity. But Melbourne thinking is epitomised by television programs like Channel 9's renovation show *The Block*, in which contestants create individualised dream homes, and subjects like 'voice activated bathrooms' are debated seriously. Rather than a utopian project, home design has become a competitive sport. As it happens, the 2016 season of *The Block* was filmed nearby on Ingles Street, Port Melbourne, in a disused commercial building.

Built in 1925, it was the administrative home of J. Kitchen & Sons, a company we've encountered several times walking the suburbs. Kitchen & Sons made Velvet Soap and Electrine candles, and was one of Port Melbourne's most significant employers for more than 150 years. Later Unilever and finally Symex, it was one of the last manufacturers to leave Port Melbourne. In the before-voice-activated-bathroom era, practically every Melbourne home contained Kitchen & Sons' soap and candles, which, as we've seen, were advertised far and wide on suburban walls. It feels fitting that, as this walk draws towards a close, we come to the source.

The transformation of the Kitchen & Sons building into apartments has attracted more attention than usual because of *The Block*. Walking past, we chat to people who have been camping outside for days, hoping to be the first allowed in when it is opened to the public. Each of the new apartments has been created by a couple whose renovation dramas have been breathlessly narrated and judged ('The judges are impressed by Dan and Carleen's motion sensor shower'.) Today's home-owning 'utopia' is a long way from the vision of Garden City, where everyone got pretty much the same house.

One could argue that at least *The Block* has resulted in the preservation and regeneration of the building rather than its demolition: a feature of the area's history has been retained, if transformed. From manufacturing to competitive renovations: there couldn't be a more symbolic example of how Melbourne has changed. There's little else left of the industry that used to go on here: besides Kitchen & Sons' offices and soap works, the 1946 Sands & McDougall lists Ryan packing case makers, Swanton & Barrett (building products), a cotton dressings factory, a plaster board factory, Canada Cycle and Motor assembly, and several other manufacturers once in business on Ingles Street. Today, while some buildings remain, other vacant blocks await the next development. Among the saw-tooth buildings, signs of trendiness have popped up: soap and packing cases have been replaced by coffee beans, avocados and pesto. You and I are twenty-first century people: with delight we home in on a café and reach for the menu. As we sip our coffee, we wonder: What kind of urban environments will the next generation inhabit? Will they be places for people to flourish, or just profit-generating machines? When a young couple looks for their first home, as we did in 1994, and those other families before us, what dreams – or nightmares – will be on offer?

COMPLETING THE CIRCLE

After two years of circumnavigating the city, we are drawing close to the end. We are completing the Melbourne circle with a walk around Port Melbourne and Fishermans Bend before returning to the point where we began.

This part of the city, on the south bank of the Yarra, bisected since the 1970s by the freeway leading to the West Gate Bridge, is very much in transition in 2016. As well as the docks, there used to be car and aircraft makers here, and other manufacturers, but many have left, and others soon will. The land has been re-zoned for housing, or is awaiting transformation into 'a techno-science-manufacturing hub', or whatever the current jargon requires. In a few years, the streetscape will have changed totally. In many parts of Melbourne, there is a strong sense of the past, but here, walking along the long wide streets between low industrial buildings and empty blocks, it's the future that is hovering, waiting to happen.

Walking south down Todd Road on a shared bike/walking trail, we come to a big red wall. At first, we are not sure what the point of it is. It can't be meant to keep people out, because there's a path that leads straight through. If anything, it fills us with a sense of intrigue about what is on the other side. (Later, we are told that the barrier is intended to reduce noise pollution from Webb Dock.) When we pass through, we reach a long straight road that takes us towards the river, with freight yards on one side and car compounds on the other. It's Sunday, not much is going on, and there are few people around to observe the odd sight of us taking our afternoon stroll beside the docks. In places the grey concrete, orange posts and painted arrows give it the feel of a Jeffrey Smart painting.

We turn back and head north up Todd Road again, making our way on foot across the busy intersection under the West Gate Bridge, where recently planted vegetation adds a welcome splash of green to the streetscape. Pedestrians are rare around here: it's one of those places where – although it's not actually forbidden – everything discourages people from being on foot. Then we hear a high-pitched, insistent buzz and whine: on our right is the Go Kart Club of Victoria. We wander in and watch for a while. A race is under way, the go karts zipping around the tracks putting us in mind of the lost greyhound track that we searched for in Tottenham a year ago.

Close to the go kart track is the Westgate Park. We have driven over it many thousands of times, but never set foot in it before. This is one of Melbourne's newest parks, created a few years ago by a community group which revegetated it with native species. Its most famous feature is a salt lake that achieves a certain celebrity every summer when it turns pink, due not (as one might think) to a chemical spill, but to algae which give off a red pigment. It's an odd feeling to be walking through bushland, around a lake, while the traffic whomps over the bridge above us. For urban people like us though, who are not really drawn to the great outdoors, this kind of bushland is ideal. As we walk, our eyes settle on tiny flowers that we can't identify, and a blue wren with flashes on its wings. Millions of winged insects zoom around us, buzzing like go karts. Although we don't know the names of the native flora and fauna (there are noticeboards telling us, which we read and instantly forget), it feels good to know that the park is here, an example of the possibilities of regeneration, like the mangroves on the other side of the river. Suddenly, from the unidentified native bushland at our feet, something whirs into life and up into the air: we look up in the hope of seeing a rare bird, but it turns out to be a drone.

Leaving the park, we explore the streets close to the water. There are rusty, overgrown railway tracks, dating from who knows when. We tramp along Lorimer Street, past cranes, silos, and a place selling show-off powerboats. There's a forlornness that emanates from factories on the verge of closing, and a sense of the next generation ready to move in: vacant blocks are adorned with real estate placards trumpeting future opportunities. The forces of growth and transformation at work across the city are cranked up to 11 in this part of town. Beside the Bolte Bridge, a number of sheds on South Wharf have been preserved: perhaps they'll undergo some kind of repurposing in the future, but the anarchist seagulls currently occupying them don't give a crap about that. We sense that whatever human beings do, the seagulls will still be here. They have their own time-scale which is nothing to do with us.

It's time to cross the river and return home. The Punt runs frequently every day between Port Melbourne and Spotswood under the West Gate Bridge, delivering passengers to a jetty just opposite Scienceworks. It's popular with cyclists and walkers who find it a convenient way to connect up with bike and walking tracks on either side. This is our first time crossing the river under, rather than over, the West Gate Bridge, and it's a short trip of barely five minutes. Ahead of us is the superb Victorian architecture of Scienceworks, originally the Spotswood pumping station, built in the 1890s as part of the Melbourne Sewerage Scheme, the great public works project of its day. In our wake are the suburbs we have spent the last few months walking through. After our big clockwise loop around the north and east of the city, we make landfall in the western suburbs again.

From here it is just a short walk back to Williamstown, where we began more than two years ago. The circle is complete. As we stand on Gem Pier, savouring the feeling of accomplishment, a restored sailing ship comes in, anachronistic among the powerboats, and symbolic of the way that in Melbourne you can't miss the co-existent presence of different time zones. A little way along Nelson Place there used to be a Victorian pub, the Oriental Hotel, which was slated for demolition. A couple of years ago, there was a fight going on to save it, and we remember it festooned in banners. Today it's a construction site and the new apartments are well advanced. Soon they will be occupied by residents who have no idea there was ever a pub here at all. It's the story of the city in miniature, played out in thousands of locations all over the suburbs.

We have also changed, during these two years. There has been loss, growth, regeneration. Increasingly, we and those around us are dealing with death – of parents, partners, friends – some sudden, others more gradual but no less cruel. Your mum passed away after several years of Alzheimer's, at the end of which the person she had once been was almost unrecognisable. Her memories gradually melted away, like old signs becoming fainter, until only a blank wall remained. A dear friend and mentor, whose witty and worldly advice guided my life, died of cancer, so too the wife of a close friend whose wedding we'd attended. People have been lost in other ways: work, distance, relationships dissolving, the erosion of time. In their place, new connections have been made, bridges built, friendships constructed on the vacant spaces of the old. Our children have grown up and left school. You have finally quit the uni where you worked for years, as it slipped ever deeper into dysfunction, and found a more sympathetic workplace. 'Hopefully this will be the start of a more positive phase,' I write in my diary. Through all the changes, the two of us continue orbiting each other like twin stars in a mutual gravity field. That's something I can count on, in 2016.

Rebecca Solnit writes: 'Places love us back ... They give continuity, something to return to, and offer a familiarity that allows some portion of our own lives to remain connected and coherent.' The city is constantly changing, and so are we, but there is an enduring connection between us and it. The more we learn of it, the more mysteries we uncover, and the stronger the connection becomes. It is not just a matter of personal cartographies – our mental maps of unique memories – that make places special, though that is part of it. It's the threads across time that we have grasped. The stories we've uncovered have taken us into the lives of others, and somehow they have enlarged us.

POSTSCRIPT

After we completed our long walk, we often talked about doing another one, or travelling to other cities, as we had when we were younger. But it didn't happen. Instead, we were thrown into the world of clinics and hospitals, waiting rooms and tests, chemo wards full of drawn anxious faces and bustling health professionals in scrubs – that particular geography known to the sick and those who love them. Our world was reduced to repeated short journeys to a few places, then just to the end of our own street, and ultimately to the four walls of the bedroom in this house where we'd lived for twenty-five years. We went on short walks for as long as we could, mainly in Williamstown, where we strolled along the foreshore again, more slowly than before, watching the windsurfers and kite flyers, joggers and dog walkers, kids playing in rock pools, pelicans posing like models on top of light poles, and ships lingering on the horizon. Once a pod of dolphins appeared out of nowhere, sporting in the waves close to the shore. When you could no longer walk, we sat together and watched the ocean. You told me you'd like your ashes scattered there, but I haven't been able to do it yet.

To my list of significant places, I have added other, unwanted landmarks: the last walk, the last coffee, the last visit to the park ... an innocent bench or parking space has the capacity to bring me to tears. I don't avoid these places – it feels as if the place knows something, as if I share you with the spots where we were together.

I guess that most people have special places like that. We keep them to ourselves, on the whole, as they are too private to share, but we carry them around in our minds: shadow cities populated by those we have lost.

I've been walking by myself again lately, revisiting the places we went together. A lot has changed already. The Champion footballer of Richmond is no longer visible from the train: tall buildings have sprouted around him like giant ruckmen. On the other hand, a statue of star AFLW player Tayla Harris in full flight launching a kick was installed at Fed Square: how you would have loved that. When I return to the places we visited during our Melbourne circle, they have another dimension: you are both there and not there, so I feel your absence, but also your presence. I remember you psychojogging alongside me, pointing out a detail I'd missed, staring up at a wall, exclaiming over some secret garden or hidden laneway.

– Look down there! How beautiful. Let's go ...

Perhaps this ability to hold presence and absence simultaneously in our minds is what gives places meaning. Something has been banked there which can be redrawn, in increments, every time we return.

It's been a year since you died and a few things have changed in the Parish of Cut Paw Paw. A house over the road has been knocked over and they're putting up apartments. They've sold the place next door where the old Greek guy lived alongside his persimmon trees. Before long, both house and trees will be gone and replaced by townhouses. In the creek, where there was a big 'pollution event' after a factory fire last year (we stood together watching the black banner of smoke unfurl across the sky, and people in white protective gear came to conduct some kind of clean-up), I recently heard frogs croaking again. Down near the Other

River, massive construction equipment has appeared and work on the new tunnel has started. Some things remain the same, though: there's an endless supply of blue-hatted kids at the primary school, replenished every year, swinging on the monkey bars, just as there are always seagulls by the ocean and possums running along our fence. I went to check out the mangroves recently: they seem to be thriving despite everything. Change and loss are everywhere, but so are survival and regeneration.

However much it changes, though, it will always be our home, freighted with memories. I'll keep an eye on things for both of us. I'll keep walking.

ACKNOWLEDGEMENTS, NOTES AND FURTHER READING

The Robert MacFarlane quote in the Prologue is from 'A Road of One's Own' in the *Times Literary Supplement* of 7 October 2005. The literature of walking is vast: just a few of the countless books about walking, memory and place that have inspired and informed this project are Rebecca Solnit's *Wanderlust, A Field Guide to Getting Lost, Infinite City: A San Francisco Atlas,* and *A Book of Migrations;* Robert MacFarlane's *The Old Ways* and *The Wild Places;* W. G. Sebald's *The Rings of Saturn*; Iain Sinclair's *London Orbital* and *London: City of Disappearances*; Nick Papadimitriou's *Scarp*; Walter Benjamin's *My Berlin Childhood*; Fritz Hessel's *Walking in Berlin* and Vanessa Berry's *Mirror Sydney.*

Besides the titles listed under specific stories below, books about Melbourne I have referred to frequently include: *The Place for a Village: How Nature has Shaped the City of Melbourne* by Gary Presland; *Melbourne Architecture* by Philip Goad; *The Rise and Fall of Marvellous Melbourne* by Graeme Davison; *Capital* by Kristin Otto; *Melbourne Art Deco* by Robin Grow; *Radical Melbourne* by Jeff and Jill Sparrow; and *Melbourne: City of Words* by John McLaren. On Melbourne signage and public typography, *Characters* by Stephen Banham is essential; on ghost signs, I recommend *Advertising and*

Public Memory: Social, Cultural and Historical Perspectives on Ghost Signs edited by Stefan Schutt, Sam Roberts and Leanne White.

I've looked up Sands & McDougall directories more times than I can recall. I mainly used the collections at the University of Melbourne's Baillieu Library and on microfiche at the State Library of Victoria.

Trove, the online resource of the National Library of Australia, is where I have found numerous newspaper articles and other bits and pieces. eMelbourne, the online encyclopedia of Melbourne, is a great source of information on most things related to the city and its history. The Australian Dictionary of Biography online (http://adb.anu.edu.au/) has provided many snippets of information. The online Victorian Heritage Register is a useful source of information about old buildings.

I also wish to thank the hundreds of people who took the time to share their thoughts and memories by commenting on my blog. Your words have enriched my understanding of Melbourne.

Williamstown: Members of Williamstown Historical Society, based at the museum, helped us find out the facts about The Beehive. References to old newspapers, here and elsewhere in the book, can be sourced via Trove.

The Sinking Village: Media coverage of this event includes 'Dreams crumbling around their ears' by Ben Hills in *The Age*, 5 September 1973. For more on Yarraville, see *Yarraville in 1901* by Carmel Taig, and *Yarraville: Village and Club* by Frances Smith.

Grand Days: For its descriptions of Footscray's cinemas in their heyday, this chapter draws on John Lack's *A History of Footscray*. Baby Guerrilla's artworks can be seen and purchased at babyguerrilla.com. Thank you to Footscray Historical Society for help and advice.

The Monkey Jockeys of White City: This chapter was informed by material in *Going to the Dogs*, a booklet by Tom Rigg published by Sunshine Historical Society. The Parliamentary quotes are taken from *Hansard*, Legislative Assembly, 6 December 1927. Thanks to Tony Birch for the tip.

Modernism and Peanut Butter: Stephen Banham's book *Characters* reproduces Romberg's architectural drawings and photos of the building in its original state. For more on Frederick Romberg, see *The Architecture of Migration*, edited by Harriet Edquist. Heritage Victoria provided information about the restoration project.

Bombs on the Maribyrnong: There is extensive detail about the explosives factories of Maribyrnong and elsewhere in David Mellor's *Australia in the War of 1939–1945*, Series 4 – Civil, Volume 5: 'The Role of Science and Industry'. John Lack's *A History of Footscray* includes much interesting material about Footscray at war. Information about Mabel Brookes and quotes are taken from her autobiography, *Crowded Galleries*. An interesting source of oral history is *When the War Came to Australia: Memories of the Second World War* by Joanna Penglase and David Horner. The Living Museum of the West has a collection of material about the munitions factories.

Sands & McDougall's Book of Everything: Some of the historical information is from *Page Not Found* by Andrew Stephens, the guide accompanying an exhibition on Sands & McDougall at the City

Gallery, Melbourne, August-December 2014.'Directories' by John Lack in eMelbourne, the online encyclopedia, provides an overview of Sands & McDougall and the other directories of Melbourne.

An Appointment with Dr King: For Melbourne doctors in the nineteenth century, see Graeme Davison's *The Rise and Fall of Marvellous Melbourne*. For quacks, see Philippa Martyr's *Paradise of Quacks: An Alternative History of Medicine in Australia*. The story of Agnes is fiction, but the newspaper advertisements are genuine: you can find them via Trove. Thanks to Gail Jones and her mother Noreen Jones (nee King) for permission to quote from correspondence and family history.

Three Ghost Signs: Thanks to Mike Alexander for information about Independent Hall.

Icons of Cremorne: More about the neon signs of Richmond and Cremorne, and Melbourne neon generally, can be found in *Characters* by Stephen Banham. More about Richmond's industries can be found in Janet McCalman's history of the suburb, *Struggletown*. For more history and some great old photos, check out the website of the Richmond and Burnley Historical Society. Thank you to the family of Vince Caponio, especially Fabrizio and Rosetta, for kindly providing information and photographs about Champion footwear. Adnate's work can be found at adnate.com.au.

Hollywood on the Yarra: I have drawn on *Homes in the Sky: Apartment Living in Australia* by Caroline Butler-Bowdon and Charles Pickett and *The Australian Ugliness* by Robin Boyd.

Lost Letters: The map of the Melbourne postal districts was published by the Deputy Director, Posts & Telegraphs in 1927. Source: State Library of Victoria.

Prahran Arcade: Thanks to the National Trust (Victoria) for access to their archives and other assistance with this story, and to Lindsay Gravina for sharing his memories of Birdland.

Three Women of St Kilda Cemetery: Biographical information in this chapter is drawn from the Australian Dictionary of Biography online. Newspaper clippings are sourced from Trove. Further information about Mabel Brookes is taken from her autobiography, *Crowded Galleries*. The cemetery publishes a handy booklet about significant graves.

City of Books: For more on Melbourne street name clusters, see *Cluster* by Stephen Banham, based on an exhibition at the City Gallery, Melbourne in 2013. On Sherwood Hall/Rothermere in Elwood, thank you to the National Trust (Victoria) for access to photos and history.

The Lost Names of Emerald Hill: Information about the names at the See Yup temple appears in 'Honouring the dead caps a life of dedication', *The Age*, 3 August 2007. The story about Barry Humphries appeared in *The Herald* in September 1966. Thank you again to the National Trust (Victoria) for assistance with photos and history of this building.

Dream Houses Past and Present: Port Melbourne Historical and Preservation Society has information about Garden City on its website: https://www.pmhps.org.au/postcards-from-port-2-housing/. The society also has a collection of Kitchen & Sons' items. For discussion of the development of Port Melbourne, see the blog Port Places by Janet Bolitho.

*

Parts of this book have previously appeared in various places and formats. I told the story of the sinking village in an essay, 'Landscape of Stories', which won the Nature Conservancy Australia Nature Writing Prize in 2015 and was published by *Griffith Review*. I wrote about the ETA peanut butter factory, the Newmarket saleyards and the Maribyrnong explosives factory in another essay, 'The Unconscious of the City', which was a finalist in the Melbourne Prize for Literature in 2015, and also published by *Griffith Review*. A version of the chapter 'Ghost signs' first appeared in *Elsewhere: A Journal of Place*. 'An Appointment with Dr King' was first published in the anthology *Melbourne Subjective*. 'The Monkey Jockeys of White City' appeared in the anthology *On the Street*.

Thanks to Jane Leonard and Kate Ryan for being supportive and insightful readers of drafts: your comments have made it a better book. Thanks again to Antoni Jach for his wisdom and advice, and the supergroupers for support; to Nick Walker and his team at Australian Scholarly Publishing for publishing the book and fulfilling his promise to 'do a nice job of it'; Jim Pavlidis for the beautiful cover; Lyn Yeowart for editing brilliance; Wayne Saunders for the expert layout; Gail Jones for kind and supportive words; Stephen Banham for many conversations about Melbourne ghost signs, Sands & McDougall, street clusters and more; and Felicity Watson at the National Trust of Australia (Victoria) for her generous assistance with several stories. I worked on parts of the manuscript while enjoying the wonderful facilities and support of Varuna: the Writers House. Thanks to Vin Maskell, who first introduced me to ghost signs. The person originally responsible for igniting my interest in psychogeography was Tony Birch, my supervisor at the University of Melbourne – this is your doing, Tony. All the errors of content, though, are mine. I wish to thank the staff of Mercy Palliative Care for their wonderful work: readers who have got this far will understand why. Thank you to Allie Meggitt. More love and thanks are due than I can express to Gabrielle, Louisa and Rosemary, and to Leanne. And infinite love as ever to Genevieve and Alicia, from both your parents.

www.ingramcontent.com/pod-product-compliance
Ingram Content Group Australia Pty Ltd
76 Discovery Rd, Dandenong South VIC 3175, AU
AUHW020922180626
428762AU00003B/27

9 781922 454072